Editor's Letter

After fifteen years of interviewing artists, designers, and creative entrepreneurs around the world, one thing has become clear to me: We need to start talking more openly about money.

We need to ask more questions. Questions like: Who is making money? Who's not—and why? What factors affect the way our work is valued, and how do those factors affect the way we spend the money we make?

The creative community seems to have a more complicated relationship with money, perhaps because we've been sold a myth that says, *If you do what you love, you'll never work a day in your life.* But even if you do what you love, and what you love happens to be something creative and untraditional, it's still work. And that work deserves to be paid.

In this issue of *Good Company*, we'll be talking about how we can better support ourselves, and our community, financially. We'll discover new ways to talk to one another about money, how to learn from shared financial mistakes *and* victories, and how to take that community knowledge and use it to inspire us all to ask for what we need.

We'll be talking about how money can make us *feel*, and how our backgrounds and identities can affect not just the way we're paid and valued but how we value money and ourselves, too. And because money isn't the only way we're paid, we'll share stories about acknowledging and appreciating the *nonmonetary* ways we are valued in our lives, too.

In addition to discussing these issues together as a community, we'll dive into the nitty-gritty. We'll guide you through everything from pricing your work as a freelancer and asking for a raise to finding ways to work toward financial independence and save for the future.

Money used to be a topic that sent me squirming to the back of my seat, but after reading these stories and unpacking some of the complicated issues that affect the way we value our work, I don't just feel like I *understand* my relationship to money more, I feel like I have better control of it. I hope all of you reading this will leave feeling inspired and empowered to not only talk about money but to ask for—and get—what you need.

Photo by Jacqueline Harriet

Contents

Contributors

Imani Barbarin

is the founder of *Crutches & Spice*, a blog that discusses the intersection of disability, race, gender, and media. While a resident of southeastern Pennsylvania, she also considers New York and Paris home. When she isn't writing, she enjoys being sarcastic toward complete strangers on Twitter @Imani_Barbarin.

Website: crutchesandspice.com
Instagram: @crutches_and_spice

Nikki Carter

is an MBA graduate, a writer/editor, and a marketer. In a prior life, she was a healthcare professional. Beyond her work with clients, she creates content under her own name in the form of articles, personal essays, and poetry. She also reads and travels when she can. She lives in San Diego with her partner.

Website: nikkim.com
Instagram: @nikitanola

Caroline Choe

is an entrepreneur, cook, artist, teacher, and writer based in New York City, and the founder of Create & Plate. Both she and her work have been featured in Jamie Oliver's *Food Revolution*, *Food & Wine*, *Food52*, *Glamour*, and PopSugar. She currently lives in the Bronx with her husband.

Website: createandplate.com
Twitter: @createandplate
Instagram: @CaroChoe

Lindsay Curtis

is an expat living in Toronto and a queer single mom to one daughter. A writer by day and a reader by night, she spends her spare time overthinking the meaning of life, tending to her indoor plants, cycling, and being with the ones she loves.

Website: curtiscommunications.org
Twitter: @LindsayWrites_

Melissa Bunni Elian

is a multimedia journalist based in New York. Her work has been published in the *New York Times*, NPR, and the *Washington Post*. Her work focuses on stories from the African Diaspora, social justice, and issues of structural inequality. Bunni currently studies at the Columbia Graduate School of Journalism.

Twitter: @bunnisays
Instagram: @hellobunni

Raven Faux

is a writer and future creative director located in the DC suburbs who's passionate about communication, compassion, diversity, and food. She enjoys listening to podcasts daily. When she's not project managing by day, she's most likely reading online articles or planning future meals.

Website: ravenousfox.tumblr.com
Twitter: @ravenous_fox
Instagram: @ravenousfox

Special thanks to Lia Ronnen, George McCalman, Aliena Cameron, Alexandria Misch, and Zach Greenwald for their support on this issue.

Andrea Gompf

is a Peruvian American writer and editor in chief of Remezcla, a leading lifestyle and entertainment media company for young Latinxs. Under her editorial leadership, Remezcla has expanded from a local-events blog to a full-fledged digital media brand. Previously, Andrea worked at one of the nation's top immigration law firms. She has a BA in literary arts from Brown University.

Website: remezcla.com

Iris Gottlieb

is an illustrator and author living in Durham, North Carolina. She brings humor and accessibility to a range of topics such as gender, science, and graphs of useless made-up data. Her clients include the *New York Times*, *Smithsonian*, Google, MTV, and the Oakland Museum of California. *Photo by Chani Bockwinkel.*

Website: irisgottlieb.com
Instagram: @irisgottlieb

Kathlyn Hart

is a financial-empowerment coach and motivational speaker who supports ambitious women. Through her salary-negotiation boot camp, Be Brave Get Paid, she helps students shift their mind-set around money so they can confidently own their worth and dare to ask for more. She is the host of the podcast *The Kathlyn Hart Show*.

Website: kathlynhart.com
Instagram: @iamkathlynhart

Lauren Holter

is a freelance reporter and editor who primarily covers politics and reproductive rights, currently based out of London. She has been published in *Bustle*, *Teen Vogue*, *Refinery29*, *Rewire.News*, and elsewhere.

Website: laurenholter.com
Twitter: @laurenholter

Kelli Hart Kehler

is the senior editor of *Good Company*, executive editor of Design*Sponge, a writer, and a journalist by trade. She managed production of Grace Bonney's book *In the Company of Women* and also manages production and edits for *Good Company*. She lives in California with her husband and two daughters.

Website: designsponge.com
Instagram: @kellikehler

Joyce Kim

was raised in the suburbs of New York and is based in Los Angeles. If she's not taking or editing pictures, she's probably hanging out with her dog or enjoying any kind of soup.

Website: joyce-kim.com
Instagram: @jokimbo

Contributors

Alora King Villa LeMalu

is a Sāmoan artist and photographer based in Oakland, California. As a DACA DREAMer and trans woman of color, LeMalu hopes that through her work, people feel given permission to peer into the struggles and joys of her realities as transparently as possible.

Instagram: @aloraloko

Amanda McLoughlin

is a podcaster, educator, and consultant from New York. She runs Multitude Productions, a collection of independent podcasts, and cohosts *Spirits*, a podcast about mythology and folklore; *Join the Party*, a collaborative role-playing and storytelling podcast; and *Waystation*, a pop culture fancast.

Website: amandamcloughlin.com
Twitter: @shessomickey
Instagram: @shessomickey

Bruna Nessif

is the author of *Let That Shit Go: A Journey to Forgiveness, Healing & Understanding Love* and founder of the website The Problem with Dating. As a Lebanese woman, she feels strongly about addressing societal and psychological effects that occur for immigrants.

Website: brunanessif.com
Twitter: @brunanessif
Instagram: @brunaaaaa

Natalie Pattillo

is a multimedia journalist based in New York City. Her work focuses on intimate-partner violence, childcare, and healthcare access, as well as food and culture. She's also a producer/writer for the documentary *And So I Stayed*, the story of Kim Brown, a domestic violence survivor.

Websites: nataliepattillo.com
  andsoistayedfilm.com

Joanna Petrone

is a writer whose work has been featured in *Popula*, *The Outline*, *Longreads*, The Awl, and the *San Francisco Chronicle*. She lives with her family in Berkeley, California, where her tomatoes don't ripen until September, and is working on a novel. Her "day job" is middle school teacher.

Twitter: @jo_petrone

Andrea Pippins

is an illustrator, designer, and author based in Stockholm. Her work has been mentioned in *O: The Oprah Magazine*, the *New York Times*, and *Essence*. Andrea is the author of *Becoming Me*, an interactive journal for young women, and *We Inspire Me*, an empowering collection of essays, interviews, and advice.

Website: andreapippins.com
Twitter: @andreagpippins
Instagram: @andreapippins

Fariha Roísín

is a writer living on Earth.

Website: fariharoisin.com
Twitter: @fariharoisin
Instagram: @fariha_roisin

Julia Rothman

is an illustrator who lives and works in Brooklyn, New York. Her drawings can be found on a variety of things from wallpaper to socks. She has written/illustrated twelve books. She also cofounded Women Who Draw, an open directory of female-identifying illustrators, artists, and cartoonists.

Instagram: @juliarothman

Kenesha Sneed

is the artist and designer behind Tactile Matter. Founded in 2014, Tactile Matter translates concepts from her design background and highlights the nuances of representation. Select clients include Saint Heron, Microsoft, and Warby Parker. Kenesha works from her Altadena, California, studio.

Website: keneshasneed.com
Instagram: @tactilematter

Jamila Souffrant

is a podcaster, writer, and founder of Journeyto Launch.com. Because of her money habits, Jamila and her husband are debt free besides their mortgage. She is also a mom of three young children and currently lives in New York City. She has been featured in *Money, Essence, Time, Business Insider,* and *Refinery29,* and on CNBC and CBS.

Website: journeytolaunch.com
Instagram: @journeytolaunch

Carlett Spike

is a writer based in Delaware but can often be found in her home state of New Jersey. Her work has appeared in a number of publications, including *UDaily* and *Columbia Journalism Review.*

Website: carlettspike.wordpress.com
Twitter: @carlettSpike

Anna Watt

is a design and technology project manager, freelance writer, and public speaker living in Seattle. She is also a cofounder of the Write/Speak/Code Seattle chapter, working to increase the visibility and leadership of women and non-binary people in tech, and helped start a Women in IT initiative at Stanford University.

Website: annalynnwatt.com
Twitter: @annalynnwatt

Why Is Money a Dirty Word?

*Group Q & A with Belinda Becker, Cora Harrington,
Walda Laurenceau & Dr. Taj Anwar Baoll*

By Natalie Pattillo & Kelli Hart Kehler
Illustration by Louisa Bertman

Money—everyone wants it, needs it, makes it, spends it, and thinks about it. But for as dominant (and often unavoidable) of a force in daily life as money is, actually talking about it is an entirely different story.

Talking about money—and what we feel we're worth—out loud and to other people can feel taboo, or uncomfortable, especially for women, people of color, and other marginalized communities. The reasons behind this are plenty: In some cultures, as Jamaican-raised DJ Belinda Becker has experienced, it is more or less forbidden for women to discuss money. Others, like The Lingerie Addict founder Cora Harrington, recognize this notion is instilled in many of us from a very early age; we're told when we're young that it's rude or impolite to talk about money, salary, and so on.

Oftentimes, when we finally get past that block and start talking about money, we reduce our worth for fear that it will be rejected—by a client, an employer, or our industry. Walda Laurenceau, a licensed acupuncturist and wellness expert, suggests identifying your relationship with money and your distinct skill set to bolster your confidence in commanding your specific rate.

But above all, it's *important* to talk about money, implores holistic business owner and motivational speaker Dr. Taj Anwar Baoll, and empower ourselves to change the way we look at needing money from a viewpoint of lacking something. And since the first step to breaking a taboo norm is making it commonplace, these four moneymaking women are here to dispel the myth that "money" is a dirty word.

As someone who is self-employed and/or has side hustles, why is it important to talk openly about money?

Belinda Becker: It's important to talk openly about money because as women we oftentimes do not get paid what we are worth. Men talk about money all the time and have no problem demanding what they want. I was raised in a family where talking about money was considered vulgar. I am from Jamaica, which has a very macho culture, where men are seen as the dominant sex and women are still looked at as weaker and needing to be taken care of. Men were allowed to talk about money among themselves but never in mixed company, and women were just not supposed to talk about it at all. But I think that is a very wrong approach. We should be raised to talk about money, our worth, and how to be able to negotiate for it. There should be classes taught in school about it. That is how we will overcome our fear and finally start to level the playing field.

Cora Harrington: There's so much confusion and shame attached to conversations about money. And anywhere there is shame and secrecy, there is also, oftentimes, exploitation and unfair treatment. Talking

*Left to right: Cora Harrington, Dr. Taj Anwar Baoll,
Walda Laurenceau & Belinda Becker*

openly about your rates, your struggles, and who is paying (or not paying) helps to unpack some of that stigma and create a better work culture for everyone.

Dr. Taj Anwar Baoll: I believe that it is important to talk about money because money is a necessity. Well, it may not be a necessity for us to be rich, but it is a necessity for us to have access to the resources that we need to thrive. For some of us, that would mean having multiple streams of income and being creative when creating those streams, and carving those niches.

Walda Laurenceau: Well, you and your skills/expertise are what you have. There is value in what you do. Getting comfortable about money and the relationship you have with it is essential. Life requires us to expend a lot of energy. Money is energy—an energy exchange for your time and service. I think—actually, I believe—that money talk begins with you examining what your needs are in order to be comfortable down to the penny so you can be better prepared when working on a project/service for a potential client. Once you get the bigger picture of the energy you are required to spend to keep you going, learn to get comfortable with stating your rates unapologetically.

Why do you think it can be scary to talk about money?

Belinda Becker: Basically because I was taught not to and women are not generally taught to know their self-worth. I still think that there are a lot of countries where men believe women are not capable of doing the same level of work as them. And this belief permeates the culture and workplace, therefore we are never encouraged to know

our self-worth or to even think we could be compensated for it in an equitable manner. A lot of us work in male-dominated fields, and that can be very intimidating. When I started as a DJ back in the late eighties, there were very few female DJs and the culture was almost completely male-driven, i.e.: male club owners, male promoters, male DJs. It took a long time for them to take me seriously. I would hear statements like, "Oh, you are a good DJ . . . for a woman." Even today, although there are many more female DJs, we still don't receive the same pay for the same work. The more I do, the easier it becomes and the better compensated I get. I don't have and have never had a manager or agent, so with the passing years I have gotten better at negotiating my fees and also positioning myself as more of an events DJ than a weekly-resident DJ. The big money is in the events. My whole philosophy is work smarter, not harder. I paid my dues doing weekly residencies. It's been a slow, steady progression with some setbacks and stumbles as with many other aspects of life.

Cora Harrington: Because we're taught, from a very young age, that it's impolite to discuss money. It's seen as rude and bad-mannered to discuss salaries, compensation, family money, help from parents, and so on. But as I mentioned before, that kind of cultural norm also creates the ideal environment for taking advantage of people, especially those from marginalized backgrounds. The only folks benefiting from that kind of secrecy are the ones writing the checks . . . not the folks receiving them.

Dr. Taj Anwar Baoll: It's scary for some people to talk about money because they live in a constant mind-set of lack. When

I say a "mind-set of lack," it means when they think of the things that they have to do, they often think about how they're going to pay for them instead of thinking how to use the resources that they *do* have access to to pay for them. We have to get away from thinking about money in terms of not having enough, and thinking in terms of how can I get what I need with what I have. If I don't have enough money, what can I do to get the money? What other resources can I obtain through other means of payment, such as bartering?

Walda Laurenceau: Fear. Fear that someone may think you are too expensive. Many of us have fallen into this mental block where we say, "Okay, maybe if I offer a super-discounted rate, they'll see how good I am." I get it, especially if you're new in the game of working for yourself. We start worrying about other people's pockets, and not enough about our own. Offering a discounted rate should be a choice, not an obligation. The hard truth is you will have to accept that some will not want to work with you simply because your rates may be higher, and that's not a bad thing. Most of the times it has nothing to do with you personally. It happens in life that you may not be able to cater to everyone and their financial situations. If it's the right fit, potential clients will find a way to make it work. Not trusting the right fit will happen is what stalls our talks about money.

In what ways can financial setbacks make you more resourceful?

Belinda Becker: Financial setbacks make you step out of your comfort zone and think of other ways of making money. Also, it becomes easier to talk about money because it becomes more of an urgent issue.

> *"Talking openly about your rates, your struggles, and who is paying (or not paying) helps to unpack some of that stigma and create a better work culture for everyone."* —Cora Harrington

Being a single mom made me more vocal about it. When you have someone depending on you, you have to put your pride and fear aside and do what you have to do to make sure that person is taken care of.

Cora Harrington: When you don't have access to traditional means of funding and raising capital, whether that's investors or family money, you have to be more creative, but I don't necessarily see that type of resourcefulness—which is incredibly stressful—as an asset. Speaking as someone who runs a bootstrap business, I often think about how much further along I could be if I had access to even a small amount of traditional funding. Because constantly hustling for cash not only chews up your time, it completely exhausts your energy—energy you would rather spend on developing your business.

Dr. Taj Anwar Baoll: When I was freshly divorced, I was so broke. I was on food stamps, Medicaid, and reduced daycare programs. I, an educated woman who I felt had earned respect, was talked to like trash while virtually begging people I didn't know, and who didn't know me, to press certain buttons so I could have access to the free resources for my family. It was belittling and demeaning, and it pushed me to never have to beg anyone for my survival ever again.

Walda Laurenceau: It's always under pressure that a diamond materializes. The sheer will to make sure the basics like rent, the lights, Wi-Fi, and food are covered is enough to keep creative juices flowing. I do believe that not caving in on yourself

is critical. Keeping your energy bright and open to receive is major; at least for me it's been successful. Know that the resources are already there and available, and using that creative force brings in that client or jobs that give you not only confidence but more settled experience for the next time.

What advice do you have for those who need help negotiating for more money for their work?

Belinda Becker: As an artist/performer, having an agent or manager negotiate for you is one way. If not, writing proposals is a good idea. And it's always best to leave a paper trail just so there is no misunderstanding about fees, equipment, et cetera. I always send a proposal and tech rider saying what I need, how much I want to be compensated, and how I want to get paid. If there is any discrepancy with fees and equipment, I always have the proposal to refer to. It basically acts as a contract. I would also recommend talking about money with other artists, friends, and people working in other fields. As women, we have to get as comfortable with our self-worth and money as men are.

Cora Harrington: Understand that it's going to be uncomfortable, especially when you start, and get okay with that discomfort. Just expect it, acknowledge it, and then plow straight through it. Negotiating does get easier over time and you do feel more confident, but neither of those things will happen if you don't start negotiating. I'd also say to think of negotiations not from an adversarial perspective

but from a collaborative one. The goal is for both of you to get what you want at the end of the deal. And if you're "negotiating" with someone who's not approaching your discussion from that perspective, then what they're looking for is not a negotiation, it's an exploitative arrangement. And it's okay to walk when you recognize that.

Dr. Taj Anwar Baoll: My advice is to increase your worth as an asset to whom you're negotiating to or carve your own niche, start a business, and be your own greatest asset.

Walda Laurenceau: I think the best thing to do first is negotiate with yourself. Lay it all down: Look at what items in your life are nonnegotiable that will give you the mental, emotional, and spiritual balance to do what you should love doing. I believe in healthy compromise. If you have to remind yourself of the time, money, and energy you had to pour into your training to justify the expertise you are bringing to the table, do that. Sometimes we tend to forget that what we are offering has tremendous value. Get comfortable with your worth and what value you are adding to someone's experience. Aim higher for you first, and work from there. Never aim lower in the hopes of landing the client, because you undermine your gifts and talents. Give yourself permission to rise to the occasion and be comfortable with saying no if something is not resonating. Remember what you're made of! **gc**

Surviving the Social Media Storm

Creative types across fields including photography, writing, food, fashion, and design weigh in on how social media has impacted their perceived worth, for good and bad.

Kelli Hart Kehler
Photo collage by Katy Edling

Social media, at first, was a slow-growing fad of an influence over modern society. You'd hear of a handful of people you knew on Facebook or Myspace—then along came Twitter and eventually Instagram, notably, and the slow burn ignited. Suddenly, it was bizarre if you came across someone who wasn't on any of the favored social platforms—social media was everywhere. Voices of those you knew and strangers alike chimed in on everything from the news to the photograph of your cousin's baby.

And then it became a crucial and essential business tool for both up-and-coming entities and cornerstones of the market. Unlike social media's birth, when there was a respectful option to sit out of participation, both the ubiquitous nature of social media and the potential for customer reach make a business's involvement in it all the more imperative.

But sharing one's business profile on these various platforms begs the need to display expertise in the field, and with that comes the risk of giving vital information away for free. Now, instead of hiring an interior designer, someone can just scroll through Instagram for design inspiration. Or maybe a cookbook sale is lost because a potential buyer thinks, "Well, I can just find that recipe on Instagram." The risk in sharing one's skill with the world, at no cost, is a frightening one to make, but the reward in building a massive following—and devoted base of customers—can make walking the tightrope worth all the near falls and the increased heart rate.

In speaking with creative types in vastly different fields, it's clear that the community-building aspect of social media might outweigh the skewed perceived notion of a particular expert's worth. Photographer Matt Armendariz, TV writer Danielle Henderson, chef Aarti Sequeira, illustrator and clothing designer Tuesday Bassen, and designer Dabito reflect on their

"I love connecting with people directly. I love that, to some degree, the playing field is leveled to allow smaller designers a chance." —Tuesday Bassen

experiences using social media to bolster their craft and followings, and how they've adapted along the way.

How do you feel social media has impacted the perceived value of your work or your community's work?

Matt Armendariz: If anything, I believe social media has increased the value of the work I do and many other professional photographers'. It's enabled us to show what happens behind the scenes, the effort and planning and scale of what it takes to make it look effortless and easy. Before, there was such an air of mystery behind food photography, even a belief that what we were doing involved fake food and sleight of hand . . . Social media has allowed us to change that conversation.

Danielle Henderson: The lovely part of social media is the attention people pay to amplifying voices, so it has certainly been useful to editors looking to find a diverse spectrum of writers. We're able to move away from the veneration of privileged systems (college, internships, nepotism) and just find people who have compelling things to say.

Aarti Sequeira: I have a love-hate relationship with it. On the one hand, I love that anyone who loves food, who loves to create food, can share their experience and creations with the world. I love that I can watch a woman in Thailand making sweet pandan noodles with coconut milk . . . and hear the birds chirping outside as she does it . . . or I can watch my friend make sheet-pan

dinners in a jiffy for her family. *But* the general lack of patience that social media causes has resulted in food that appeals to only one dimension of our tastebuds—covered in cheese or in rainbows. And I find that limitation frustrating. Social media has created "Instagram food," which appeals to the eye but is not a pleasure to eat.

Tuesday Bassen: I'm not quite sure how to measure perceived value, especially in an industry like fashion that has devalued anything that isn't thin, white, and able-bodied. To be frank, I'm not looking for the approval of the fashion industry, but am instead looking to forge new paths, new approaches in fashion, and meaningful connections with people.

Dabito: The great thing about social media is that it builds a community and brings awareness to a lot of things—either it's societal issues or domestic ones, like tackling your own bathroom makeover. There's definitely value in that. I feel really lucky that I get to create my dream spaces and share them on social media and see that it inspires other people to have fun creating their own.

How has the demand for your work changed in recent years? Do you see any correlation between that demand and your social media presence?

Matt Armendariz: I don't think the demand has changed so much as the scope of the work. I have been hired based on my social media presence for photo gigs and photography-related events. But then

again, my photo career began because of blogging, so they kind of came up together, so maybe it's hard for me to know where I'd be without social media!

Danielle Henderson: I branched out into three different writing careers simultaneously (which I do not recommend!)—writing books, writing television shows, and developing television shows—but they all had very little to do with my social media presence. Social media was *much* more useful when I was a freelance writer. None of my current jobs are based on the number of Twitter followers I have (or if they are, my bosses keep that information to themselves).

Aarti Sequeira: I do think there's a direct correlation between getting gigs and how many people "follow" you . . . whether that's actual TV work or endorsement work. What used to be a bonus that you could offer to a potential employer is now the basis upon which you get work! It's tough. I see social media as a way to connect with my supporters, to show them a less polished version of myself, and to let them know what I'm up to, professionally and personally. It's a very pure communication, and the payoff for me is that I have very interactive, loyal fans. I'm trying to figure out how to honor that relationship now whilst also being open to the ever-changing nature of this business.

Tuesday Bassen: Four years ago, I was exclusively known as an illustrator. I was working hard to express my ideals through client and personal work, but I made the conscious shift to creating useful items so I could be my own art director and reach my audience directly. In 2015, I started making a few clothing items based on my artwork. In 2019, my notoriety and energy is focused almost solely on my ethically made, size-inclusive, eponymous clothing line. My social media presence has been intrinsically tied to the shifts in my career.

Dabito: Demand for my work has definitely grown because of my social media presence. There's definitely more exposure and in return, more work!

Have your fees or pricing structure changed in response to social media demand or impact?

Matt Armendariz: A bit, yes. There are jobs that are smaller in scale and pay, meant directly for social media. However, I've also been paid full-day rates for shooting social. But it can be all over the board, just the way it can be for standard photo shoots that depend on usage, geography, and timelines for pricing.

Danielle Henderson: At the end of my freelance career, I had enough courage to ask for a little more money from some publications, but that had more to do with my desire to survive New York City. I don't think I could ever ask someone for more money based on social media demand—I don't have the self-esteem for it.

Aarti Sequeira: Again, this is something I'm working with my team on. I'm in the midst of a rehab that, beyond the

aesthetics, is also a long-overdue recognition that I need to take myself seriously and believe in myself! It's tricky: I want to help out my friends and colleagues who are launching their own products . . . but I also need to provide for my own family!

Tuesday Bassen: Honestly, I've never been good at pricing my own work and prefer the pricing structure of clothing sales. It feels like a concrete way to get paid what I think I should versus haggling my worth with other companies. Now that my clothing line is in a good place with a great team, I'd love to diversify my practice and bring in more illustration work again. When I do, I plan to reach out to a few friends to better understand pricing structures in the industry. Don't be afraid to ask your peers for advice!

Dabito: My pricing is always based on the scope of work. That being said, my pricing often changes because social media keeps evolving.

Do you feel that social media has had, overall, a positive or negative impact on your work and finances as an artist?

Matt Armendariz: Absolutely positive! I know there are some photographers who tend to see social media as watering down what we do ("Everyone has a camera! Everyone is a photographer!"), but I definitely do not buy into that mode of thinking. Social media has allowed me to reach a greater audience, has allowed me to share what I do behind the scenes, and has opened up so many doors for me. It's also

been a way to monetize opportunities that didn't exist previously!

Danielle Henderson: Overall positive—it definitely connected me to people doing interesting work, and helped reinforce the importance of community when you're building a career.

Aarti Sequeira: Positive. My strength has always been in connecting to people on a very real level . . . warts and all. Being able to show that numerically is helpful for me.

Tuesday Bassen: Absolutely positive. Instagram allowed me to explore personal work with an audience and eventually gave me the forum to grow as a clothing designer. We (my team and I) spend almost no money on advertising, and connect directly with people who are looking for size-inclusive, slow fashion.

Dabito: Social media has been a positive experience for me. I've met some really wonderful people who I learned a lot from by working together. I'm also really grateful that I get to create content, share it on social media, and get paid for it. It's been an interesting journey. I hopped on social media in 2010 and didn't start making legit money from it until 2015. So it wasn't like an overnight thing.

What are your favorite and least favorite parts of social media (when it comes to your work)?

Matt Armendariz: My favorite part would be the ability to connect, engage, ask questions, and offer advice. We are a community of food lovers, tech lovers, travel lovers, and it's literally so amazing to be able to reach so many people and begin a discussion. My least favorite parts would have to be that it can sometimes distract us from what is right in front of us, and it can overamplify our minds when we sometimes need to take it down a few notches. Or maybe that's just me!

Danielle Henderson: It's a wonderful way to find people who may be interested in TV writing but have no concrete way in. I came to this field in a really backward, luck-filled way (my reps found me because they liked my TV recaps). When the time comes to hire people to work on my own shows, social media is going to be a huge part of finding writers who have personality. You can teach someone how to structure a script; you can't teach them how to be funny. My least favorite part: Social media has really raised the stakes for validation-seeking behavior. Everyone knows they can be seen, so there's a performative element that kind of freaks me out.

Aarti Sequeira: Trying to figure out ways to talk about products in a way that doesn't make me feel inauthentic.

Tuesday Bassen: I love connecting with people directly. I love that, to some degree, the playing field is leveled to allow smaller designers a chance. I enjoy constructive comments and requests from customers. I

don't feel like I struggle very much with boundaries or hateful or harassing comments from our customers, and that is a blessing.

Dabito: My favorite part is that I get to collaborate with talented people and work with some really major brands. It's crazy and I'm beyond grateful! And the best part is that I typically have full creative control, which is the best thing ever! My least favorite part is probably when it comes to dealing with the value of my work. When I feel like it's being undervalued by clients, it's never a great feeling. But I've learned to say no to work when that happens.

What is a challenge you faced and overcame as a result of adjusting to a more social media–aware society? What did you do differently?

Matt Armendariz: Apart from having to have a life that is 100 percent camera-ready at all times? I'm joking, but also a bit serious! I think the biggest challenge is when I'm working, and everyone is sharing and snapping in real time. I certainly don't mind, but it can be distracting when I'm trying to work and want my team as well as my client to be present and focused on what we are doing. I understand that the client wants to share the process, but it's distracting nonetheless. Of course all this is solved when we have social media blackouts (new products, exclusivity, et cetera), but that's not very often. People want to share!

Aarti Sequeira: Posting when I don't feel like it. Having some photos banked for these sorts of days helps a lot!

Tuesday Bassen: Social media is truly a wonderful tool for better understanding the perspective of someone different from yourself. I try to absorb, understand, and apply any teachable moments to my own business and personal practice. I challenge myself to be the best leader I can be, and a large part of that is taking criticism to heart, whether it's for me or another person. I'm not ashamed to say I was wrong or that I can try harder next time, but it is absolutely my responsibility to follow through and do so.

Dabito: Social media can feel like this popularity contest. And there's this weird pressure to constantly share. I try to block that out. I've learned to not let that dictate how and when I want to share anything. But at the same time, with a more social media–aware society, everyone should be more mindful of how you're sharing content. There needs to be some sort of social-sharing integrity.

What advice would you have for someone who feels like their work or services are being devalued or overshadowed by social media?

Matt Armendariz: I'd say the issue that is causing you to feel devalued or overshadowed isn't social media. It's simply a thing

> "*Social media can feel like this popularity contest. And there's this weird pressure to constantly share. I try to block that out. I've learned to not let that dictate how and when I want to share anything.*" —Dabito

(social media), and the focus should be on creating the best work you can do. It's that simple. Spend the energy becoming the artist you want to be, and if you do this with integrity, honesty, and self-value, then it will always be recognized. Always.

Aarti Sequeira: Try to find other people in your field and analyze their profiles . . . look at what they post, how often, how they interact with their followers. That is the best course you can take!

Tuesday Bassen: There is often no better advocate for you than yourself. I'd consider the following: Are there alternate routes or can you shift gears to better serve your goals? Have you been transparent about your feelings? Are you being true to yourself with what you're presenting to others? What does being valued look like to you?

I try to measure success not by follower count (though let's be real—it's a bummer to stagnate!), but what my goals are personally, outside of feedback from others. Easier said than done, but it keeps me in a good mental place.

Dabito: Social media is this really strange universe, right? And it can feel like your work is being overshadowed by a sea of creatives. But that's also true in the real world. My advice is don't let anything stifle your creativity. Continue to create work and keep sharing it, even if you feel like nothing is happening. I've definitely

felt like my work wasn't good enough at some point. Don't compare yourself or your work to anyone else's. You have to believe in yourself and put in the time and effort into making and creating. To me, it's like planting seeds or investing. Nothing might come out of it at the moment, but it'll grow and you'll grow and hopefully blossom into something worthwhile, and that might take one, two, or even five years. You have to be patient and tenacious. Take your work to the next level. And absolutely demand your worth. If you don't know your worth, I always recommend talking to people who have more experience. It's a crazy (social) world, and we're here to help each other navigate it.

How do you see social media shaping the future of your work or career path?

Matt Armendariz: I would hope that my career as a photographer or whatever I do in the future would grow alongside social media. It's so ingrained in what I do now that it's a part of me. I'm quite happy to be in this space, so wherever it takes me will be an adventure!

Danielle Henderson: I'm in the process of retreating from social media. It's challenging to be a person who both values their privacy but also enjoys connecting to people, and I just don't think social media is helpful for developing healthy boundaries. I know that it's a privilege to be able to step away—right now, my livelihood doesn't

depend on my social media activity. My ultimate goal is to move to the woods, so I would be happy if social media had no impact on the future of my work at all.

Aarti Sequeira: I'm excited by it because I'm passionate about authenticity . . . whether it's in recipes or in storytelling (I was a producer at CNN before this world). And while social media poses a *very* real danger of sharing only the high-light reel, I am focused on sharing the harder parts, too, so we can all feel a little less lonely in the reality of life.

Tuesday Bassen: That's a great question. I think we're beginning to see a shift away from Instagram culture, and I can't wait to see what's next.

Dabito: I feel like it's already shaped so much of my career. It has helped me explore what I love to do and helped me focus on what I want to do. **gc**

Making Your Own Path and Getting Paid

Comedian, actress, and writer Quinta Brunson shares how she learned to have a better relationship with money after going broke early in her career.

By Carlett Spike
Photography by Kayla Reefer

Quinta Brunson's viral beginnings stem back to her 2014 Instagram series The Girl Who's Never Been on a Nice Date. With each view, comment, and like, Brunson jumped on the opportunity to find a way to profit off this new territory and launch her career. Since then, she has hustled on many stages from stand-up comedy to videos like *Broke*, a series she created and starred in for YouTube Red.

Trial and error helped her to establish a healthy relationship with money in an unconventional field of work. Brunson has now broken into TV comedy with this year's announcements that she will star in the CW's *The End of the World as We Know It* and be one of the stars and executive producers on *Quinta & Jermaine* for CBS. She's also working on her first book, *She Memes Well*.

Brunson spoke with *Good Company* about making money through her multiple passions, what she learned after going broke, and dealing with others' undervaluing of her talent.

Can you start off by telling me how you describe your work?

Quinta Brunson: I would describe myself as a writer, actress, and comedian.

Your viral beginnings stem back to your Instagram dating series. Reflecting on it now, did you ever imagine making money when you came up with the idea?

QB: I knew I had the potential to have a career in comedy and writing already

We just really all have to give ourselves the room to fail, and we have to understand the importance of failing and realize it's not the end of the world . . .

because that was what I was going for. So that was going to happen one way or another. With my first viral video, I saw the opportunity to monetize within my career in a different way than I had sought out before.

So can you share your thought process about how to make money off Instagram?

QB: The internet just presented a new outlet. I wasn't necessarily interested in doing viral videos, period, but I saw an opportunity there. So, one of the first ways that I monetized my career was by selling T-shirts with catchphrases from the videos on them. It taught me a lot about making money in that way, because it takes a team if you want to do it right. It then involves another skill set of record keeping and business management.

Can you talk more about the business aspect of it and highlight what skills you had to learn?

QB: It's not as simple as, "Oh, people are paying me for T-shirts." No, now you have to get T-shirts out to people in time, which is record management. Making sure you have enough product to manage demand. Setting up how you're going to do your business so that you can still live your life, too, because most companies that sell T-shirts have workers. I didn't have that. I only had myself and friends. So I had to manage my time as well, to make sure my business didn't become only selling T-shirts. Eventually if you're making

too much money, whoever you're going through wants a cut of it, and to protect yourself you need to start understanding taxes and what kind of business you're operating. A lot of it is about having the foresight to protect yourself from things that can come in the future. So it took a lot of reading and learning about that part of it because my background was in communications and advertising, it wasn't in business management.

You've previously mentioned you went broke. Can you talk about what happened and what advice you would give to creatives who don't get regular paychecks?

QB: It taught me that I need to learn how to manage large amounts of money instead of continuing to go down that path of, "Okay, well, oh no! I made $20,000 and now it's all gone. I need to make another $20,000 quickly." That's cute and all, that sounds like a large sum of money, but in reality it's not. So, for me I think stability is key and I wish a lot more young creatives out there understood that. That was part of the reason I got my job at BuzzFeed. So, my advice is just understand the importance of stability and making a weekly income.

Describe your three years at BuzzFeed. Can you reflect on your transition from the residency program to eventually becoming a development partner?

QB: Part of my job description was to make viral videos. To me, it wasn't just about

viral videos, it was about making narrative pieces that would be shared well. So I really just enjoyed doing it and finding new ways to tell stories in the digital world. When I started there, there was no such position as a development partner, so that role was formed out of the work that I and others did. I think it was a very rare opportunity to be a part of creating new positions and creating new divisions of a company, not only as a young person or a Black woman, but it's a really rare opportunity period for anyone. I loved my time there and growing there.

When did you know it was time to move on?

QB: It's just like any other job. You're at your job and it's just like, "Okay, I want to do something else now." It really was that simple. If I could no longer be a good employee here and I can't do my job to the best of my ability, then that means it's time to move on.

What choices did you make financially to prepare for the transition?

QB: I had savings and this time I had a better relationship with money, because it's freelancing and I don't know when I'll get paid. It's really about being conscious with spending, no matter what. It's so funny because I think a lot of people think once you have a lot of money—whatever that means, because that means different things to different people—that all your spending troubles go away. You really have to pay attention to every little detail. I hate it. It's like a second job, but it's so important.

. . . Failure is a part of life. Just because you fail at something does not mean that's over for you. You can still keep going.

I think one challenge creatives face is labels (you're a writer or you're just a singer, et cetera). Can you talk about pitching different ideas and selling yourself with multiple talents?

QB: I think that the best thing we can do, even if it's frustrating, is just to continue to do what we believe we're good at. I really try not to get upset about what people see me as because I will never be able to control the way the world sees me. I actually started to look at it as a bonus that I can go anywhere and be anything at any given time. I think that's really fun. I try to always remember that I'm young and I can do whatever the hell I want. Tomorrow if I want to be a pilot, I can go become a pilot. All it is is getting your pilot's license and acting on it.

That's true! I think for many people it can be hard to stray once they set a path because then it feels like failure.

QB: I'm glad you brought up failure because that's the other part of it. We just really all have to give ourselves the room to fail, and we have to understand the importance of failing and realize it's not the end of the world. Failure is a part of life. We hear it all the time, but we keep ignoring it. Just because you fail at something does not mean that's over for you. You can still keep going.

Since you do wear so many hats, what is the most challenging part of your job?

QB: Management. Making sure I'm focused on the right things at the right times. Sometimes I get wrapped up in a certain project and I'll let other things fall to the wayside, but that's not really fair because I've committed. So the hard part is definitely managing my focus.

What is the hardest part about financially supporting yourself that people may not realize?

QB: I think that for my career people might not realize it's not always about making money. Sometimes it's about making the right decision for five years later in your future. People may not understand why we turn down a certain opportunity, especially if there is a lot of money involved. Money does not equate to happiness. It's important to set those boundaries. Often, too, many people think just because a person isn't flashy means they don't have good income. I save a lot.

What advice do you have for others who are struggling to explain their career choices to loved ones?

QB: I think that they should have honest conversations. I just started having very honest conversations with my parents about what I wanted and why. You may have something to learn from their perspective, too. My parents helped me a lot with thinking about the bigger picture and saying things like, "Well, if you're going to do this, how will you handle having a retirement plan?" Those questions may seem trivial, but they are not. You may not always agree at the end, but you can't always ask for agreeing. Sometimes all you can ask for is listening and learning.

Early this year, comedian Mo'Nique reignited conversations about equal pay after claiming Netflix offered her less money because she is a Black woman. Do you find that you deal with similar issues of people not valuing you for what you know you're worth?

QB: Yeah. If you're a part of a marginalized community, it's a difficult thing to deal with, and even if you surpass that, there's still going to be instances of people not knowing your value or not paying you what you're worth. Let's say Mo'Nique and Netflix, maybe Netflix did not see her being as valuable as she actually is. I think being a Black woman is part of it, but there's a lot of other different reasons. There's cultural relevance, who's going to actually bring eyes in with their names, and all of that intersects in different areas. I think it's really tough when we give it a blanket statement.

So what do you do in those situations? How do you personally handle it?

QB: If I feel like a place isn't valuing me in the correct way, I just walk and move on to somewhere else that will. I tend to handle things pretty simply and I don't want commotion. I don't really see the need to

convince someone. Even if I really feel like someone is missing out on an opportunity, that's fine. I would rather go to a place where I'm not missing out on the opportunity and build.

Do you have advice for young creatives who are looking to pursue a path that many see as unconventional?

QB: It's not always easy, which we all know, but if you have a strong will for what you're doing, I think that is something that really keeps me going. It keeps me going, but that doesn't necessarily keep me sane. You are going to go insane sometimes, so get ready. The world we chose, you have to be comfortable with that. You're not a bad person because you have a flip-out every once in a while. Also, I know savings is not always easy for people to acquire, but if you can have savings, it just helps so much. If I can save someone from having to learn that hard lesson I would like to. You should definitely have savings, it's important. **gc**

WOMEN ON MONEY

Words + pictures by Julia Rothman

No portraits of women appear on American dollar bills. During the Obama presidency, a nonprofit grassroots organization called Women on 20s hoped to change that. They launched a campaign to get a woman on the $20 bill by 2020, the centennial of the 19th Amendment, which gave women the right to vote. Their efforts were successful and on April 20, 2016, then-Treasury Secretary Jack Lew officially announced that Andrew Jackson would be replaced by abolitionist Harriet Tubman on the front of the $20 bill. But in August of 2017, Treasury Secretary Steven Mnuchin said he wasn't committed to carrying out the change, stating, "Right now we have a lot more important issues to focus on."

Other countries have had notable women appear on their currency for decades. Here are some of my favorites:

<u>Débora Arango</u>   B. 1907 D. 2005   COLOMBIA

In her paintings and other works, Colombian artist Débora Arango often portrayed political charged and controversial imagery. Her pieces depict the role of women in society and featured less commonly seen subjects like prostitutes and victims of political violence.

PROMISE TO PAY THE BEARER ON DEMAND THE SUM OF K200

RESERVE BANK OF MALAWI

ISSUED UNDER THE RESERVE BANK OF MALAWI

200 KWACHA

200 KWACHA

AL 6141460

Rose Chibambo

B. 1928 D. 2016   MALAWI

Chibambo was a politician and activist in the Protectorate of Nyasaland, a British territory in Africa. She coordinated efforts to fight for the independence of Malawi and became the first woman minister in the new cabinet.

Fatma Aliye Topuz

B. 1862 D. 1936   TURKEY

Topuz is credited as the first woman, Muslim, professional novelist of the Ottoman Empire. She was also a women's rights activist and founded a charity to help support families of soldiers.

TÜRKIYE CUMHURIYET MERKEZ BANKASI

B 129 650359

ELLI TÜRK LIRASI

50

R 129 650359

AA06833084 საქართველოს ეროვნული ბანკი

FIFTY LARI

50

50

AA 06833084

Tamar the Great B. 1160 D. 1213   GEORGIA

Queen Tamar was the first woman to rule Georgia. She came to power in 1184 and helped expand the kingdom. The time period she reigned is known as the Golden Age in Georgian history.

Las Hermanas Mirabal ↗

B. 1924 1926 1935 D. 1960   DOMINICAN REPUBLIC

Patria, Minerva, and Maria Teresa are "feminist icons" in the Dominican Republic. They opposed the dictatorship of Rafael Trujillo, aka El Jefe, and led a rebellion against him. Known to some as "Las Mariposas" (the butterflies), they distributed pamphlets, made weapons and makeshift bombs. In 1960, the sisters were assassinated by the regime. But since their deaths they have been commemorated in many ways. Notably, the United Nations General Assembly assigned November 25, the day of their death, in their honor as the International Day for the Elimination of Violence Against Women.

Carmen Lyra ↗

B. 1888 D. 1949   COSTA RICA

Lyra was the first prominent woman writer and was the founder of the first Montessori school in Costa Rica, for the preschool education of low-income infants. She was also one of the founders of the Communist Party of Costa Rica as well as a union for women workers.

Juana de Ibarbourou ↘

B. 1892 D. 1979   URUGUAY

One of the most famous Latin American poets, Ibarbourou's poems contain themes of love, nature, feminism, and eroticism.

Nanny of the Maroons ↑

B. 1686   D. 1755   JAMAICA

Nanny is officially a "Jamaican national hero" and has become a powerful symbol of the Maroon resistance to slavery. She settled and controlled Nanny Town, farming and trading peacefully away from European settlements. According to oral accounts, she had magical powers that allowed her to protect Maroons from British bullets. She helped free hundreds of slaves.

Dido ↓

B. 839 BC   D. 759 BC   TUNISIA

Dido was the first queen of Carthage, the Phoenician state, according to Greek legend. She appears in the Aeneid, a story by the Roman poet Virgil.

Emmy Destinn

B.1878 D.1930   CZECH REPUBLIC

Before WWI, Destinn was one of the most famous sopranos. She sang all over Europe and at New York's Metropolitan Opera House. Her voice was exceptionally powerful and rich.

Adela and Celsa Speratti →

B.1865-1902, 1868-1938   PARAGUAY

The Speratti sisters were responsible for advancing the education system of Paraguay by developing new teaching methods and increasing opportunities for girls and women.

Kate Sheppard   B.1848 D.1934   NEW ZEALAND

Sheppard was a prominent figure in New Zealand's women's suffrage movement. She was editor of the country's first women-run newspaper, and her pamphlets like "Ten Reasons Why the Women of New Zealand Should Vote," helped persuade the public opinion. She was the first president of the National Council of Women of New Zealand.

한국은행

오만 원

50000

한국은총재

50000

AC 0555460 J

50000

AC 0555460 J

NCO CENTRAL
L. PARAGUAY
BANCO CENTRAL DEL PARAGUAY
RECONOCE ESTE BILLETE POR
000
- GUARANIES
O 2011
PRESIDENTE
C 1329 4731

Banco de México

Quinientos Pesos

500

500 Pesos

Shin Saimdang

B.1504 D.1551   SOUTH KOREA

Aside from being known as a painter, writer, and calligrapher, Saimdang was also known as a "wise mother" and "gifted at fulfilling a wife's role." She had seven children. When it was decided her image would appear on the banknote, feminists criticized the selection. They felt she was not someone who should represent gender equality.

Frida Kahlo   B.1907 D.1954   MEXICO

A celebrated feminist artist, Kahlo's folk-style surreal paintings explore identity, race, class, and gender in Mexican society. Many of her paintings are self-portraits. She identified as bisexual and a Communist.

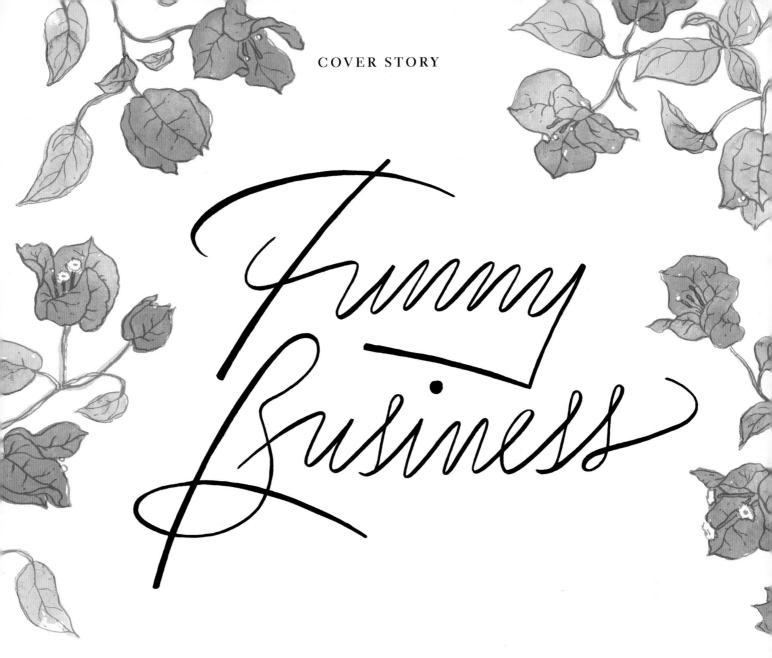

Funny Business

Comedian, writer, and actress Aparna Nancherla
finds stability and builds community—onstage and off.

Interview by Grace Bonney
Photography by Joyce Kim
Styling by Natalie Toren
Hair by Taylor Tanaka
Makeup by Afton Williams

I don't want to become a one-note thing or like, this is my whole *deal*, because we're all three-dimensional people, and we want to be more than just our demons.

"Listen, I'd love to stop and chat, but I have crippling social anxiety."

"Wherever my depression is right now, I hope it's happy."

"Isn't therapy just a podcast off the record?"

One-liners like these are precisely why comedian Aparna Nancherla's sense of humor is so instantly relatable and beloved. Her distinctive blend of dry, slightly absurd, and thoroughly honest humor taps into our society's collective well of anxiety and depression. What Nancherla is able to do that so many of us struggle with is to give a voice (and some lightness) to our shared struggles with mental health.

And while the cliché of the slightly neurotic, overthinking comedian is nothing new, there is something *different* about these conversations and stories in the hands of Nancherla. She has an awareness of their power to bring people together *and* their risk of limiting people to a one-dimensional representation. And she's working to move beyond those one-note ideas of comedians toward a more evolved and three-dimensional representation of not just *herself*, but of others in her community.

Open Mic Night in Northern Virginia
Nancherla grew up in the suburbs of Washington, DC, in McLean, Virginia, where her parents, both doctors, emigrated from India in the late 1970s. She had what

she described as a "pretty typical upper-middle-class upbringing," and she and her older sister were, at the urging of their parents, highly school-oriented and excelled at extracurricular activities like piano lessons and dance classes.

While Nancherla admits that comedy was, "sort of a curveball career move" for her, there *were* early signs that comedy held a power she would find useful later in life.

Every week Nancherla and her sister attended what she calls "Hinduism Sunday School." It was there that she took a public speaking class and realized the power of humor. "I entered a speech competition. I remember I made my speech *funny*, and everyone else's was a bit more serious and political. I think I tried to take down Bollywood movies or something. I was like, "So . . . this is my problem with Bollywood movies." I think because it was *funny*, it stood out from the other ones and I ended up winning. That was probably the first time where I realized: I like making people laugh in front of a big group. That felt more comfortable to me than a lot of things that were more mundane, like talking to people at a party. I felt like I had a sense of control. I think that planted the seed."

After this realization, Nancherla would try to work jokes into her school presentations or write them in a humorous way. But it wasn't until college, when a friend suggested they check out an open mic night at a comedy club in Tyson's Corner, Virgnia, that she tried her hand at comedy onstage.

"[My friend] was like, 'I'm going to try this open mic,' so I thought, I guess I could try that too. I think it went well enough that I thought *maybe* I could put this on the back burner for the future, because I didn't try it again until after I graduated from college and moved back home. But that definitely was my first real dip into the water."

Next Steps

After graduating from Amherst with a degree in psychology, Nancherla got her first real set onstage and spent the summer preparing for it. "There was a *lot* of overthinking involved in it. I tried to write ideas for material the whole summer. I wrote about living with my parents and summer jobs. But it was pretty basic and I truly did not know what I was doing. I put off the set until the very end of the summer. I think my first set was actually *on* my birthday, so I definitely mentioned that during the set. 'Please be nice. It's my birthday and my first time onstage.'"

Nancherla continued doing stand-up sets on a regular basis while living at home with her family. She continued to build her act—and confidence—onstage while working temporary jobs around town. In 2012 she moved to New York City, where she was offered a full-time job writing for the television show *Totally Biased with W. Kamau Bell* in New York City. It was in writer's rooms like this that Nancherla discovered one of the best parts of working in comedy and comedy writing. "My favorite part of my job is being creative and getting to meet people who see the world in an offbeat way. With TV writing you're essentially telling a story and finding an interesting or a funny way to tell it. That has been really cool and so exciting to get to do with a group of people."

After her time on *Totally Biased*, Nancherla wrote for NBC's *Late Night with Seth Meyers*. Soon after, comedian Tig Notaro (whom Nancherla had met while performing at a comedy festival Notaro started in Washington, DC) encouraged her to create a comedy album. And in 2016, Nancherla's debut album, *Just Putting It Out There*, was released on Notaro's label, Bentzen Ball Records.

Full-Time Funny Business

Going on her seventh year of full-time comedy work, Nancherla understands that part of any successful career is trying different avenues and forms of comedy. In addition to stand-up and writing for television series, Nancherla has created a podcast (*Blue Woman Group*, about depression, with Jacqueline Novak) and a web series (*Womanhood*, with Jo Firestone for *Refinery29*) and has done voice work for shows like *BoJack Horseman* and *Steven Universe*. She's also appeared on television shows such as *Master of None* and films like *A Simple Favor*, and is a regular on the Comedy Central show *Corporate*.

With all of the avenues she's pursuing as her work evolves, Nancherla is aware that she needs to be careful not to overdo it. "I think for me personally the hardest part of what I do is balancing self-care with feeling like I'm doing enough in terms of making my career happen. I have a big fear of letting people down. I think once you become responsible for other people's incomes, whether it's through them representing you or not feeling your best and wanting to cancel [an appearance], you have to learn how to prioritize what you show up to and how and when you're saying yes to things."

Nancherla is aware that *no one* can do all of these projects alone. She has a supportive team around her, including friends like comedy writer Joe Zimmerman and comedians such as Sarah Silverman and Tig Notaro, and is careful to acknowledge that all of the brightest moments we see from the outside are the result of a team effort. "You may be the face of a project as the artist, but depending on what it is, there are *so* many different pieces of a puzzle that all come together. In the end, it may seem like it's your thing because your face is on it and you're the one promoting it heavily, but everything is because you're part of a *team* of people who are helping to create that thing. You're always a piece of a bigger thing and someone is helping you engineer your vision."

Mental Health and Comedy

Anxiety, depression, and mental health are a big part of Nancherla's comedy, but she's aware of how easy it is to get trapped in those concepts as identities. "I've sort of wrestled with whether it helps or hurts [to be known for those topics], because once it becomes your full-time career and your livelihood, your relationship to them changes. I don't want it to become a one-note thing or like, this is my *whole* deal, because **we're all three-dimensional people, and we want to be more than just our demons**."

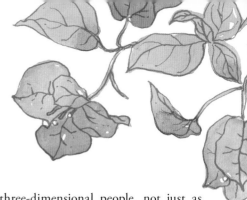

"The reason I started talking about this in the first place was I was kind of in a rut creatively. It felt like depression and anxiety were kind of exacerbating that or maybe even the *cause* of that rut. I think talking about them became a way to take some of the power out of it or work through what I was dealing with at the time. I think now I'm trying to find a balance between talking about it and not letting it dominate everything."

Nancherla mentioned the impact comedian Hannah Gadsby's special, *Nanette*, had on her work and perception of mental health and comedy. In *Nannette*, Gadsby questions how comedy and punch lines can trap comedians in negative relationships with their identities and stories. "I think it made me think about what is the goal of comedy a lot of times," she explained. "Who are you really trying to lighten the mood for? Is it for other people, or is it for yourself? I think it is a very fine line between making light of stuff that a lot of times can be very painful or dark, and trying to figure out what exactly you are trying to say at the end of the day."

Identity

Working toward a more three-dimensional representation of herself and her comedy, Nancherla has tested a lot of platforms for her work, especially social media. And while it can be a powerful incubator, she's aware of the risks.

"I think social media has exacerbated the idea that you're freely inspired at all times, especially with Twitter, where you're writing jokes. Sometimes people will be like, *I didn't like this tweet*, or *This wasn't your best tweet*, or something. You're like, Okay, but this is free content and I'm not really trying to [present this as] a finished, fully polished joke. But people are like, *I get to be the arbiter of whether I like this or not.*" And that feedback can be complicated when the issues of identity are involved.

"Right now in the comedy community, there is this idea that if you're not a straight white male, it's like, *Oh, lucky you*. Like if you're a woman of color that's all people want right now. But, *no*. I think it's just correcting an imbalance that has existed forever, and it might seem that way because we're not used to paying attention to people who have traditionally been on the margins. People think I must be rolling in opportunities right now. But with that comes that thing of, well, everyone also has their own agenda they're projecting onto you. **And at the end of the day, you can really only follow your own intuition as to what projects you want to do. You have to navigate your humanity within all the politics of what's marketable or what's trending at the moment.**"

The Future

Nancherla's keen observation of feedback on social media and trends in comedy has given her a sharply honed barometer of who and what she can trust as her career evolves. "I think I'm more sensitive to this now, because it feels like there's more opportunity for people based on their identity right now. But at the same time, you don't want to be pigeonholed. I think the good thing about it is that [the industry] is asking for those voices, but

as three-dimensional people, not just as whatever that one identity is."

As Nancherla moves forward she has her eyes on a more holistic and realistic view of her work and the industry as a whole. "There's one saying that I always turn to: 'Don't compare your behind-the-scenes to someone else's highlight reel.' I love that quote, because I do exactly that. I always see people's high points, and I'm like, why can't I just do that? But I'm not seeing any of the stuff going on right in the background."

In a world where we're all just doing our best to be seen and heard as full people, Nancherla's open-eyed and openhearted view of comedy (and creative life) serves us all well. Understanding that everyone is struggling behind the scenes, doing their best, and hoping to do something that makes people smile is a great reminder for life *and* work.

And at the end of the day, Nancherla is just hoping to make people laugh. When I asked her who she would most want to enjoy a set of hers, she said, "Grover from *Sesame Street*. I would love to have a conversation with a Muppet to begin with, but I think if I then got to imagine Grover sitting in the audience and listening to the whole show, I think I could subsist off of that for a long time." **gc**

ASHLEY NICOLE BLACK

Interview by Natalie Pattillo
& Kelli Hart Kehler

The comedian, actress, and television writer/correspondent for Full Frontal with Samantha Bee *has found financial support through her comedy career, but it wasn't always this stable. She found out early in her career that backing up her comedy work with a second stream of income allowed her the creativity and peace of mind to put forth her best work.*

How has financial stability (or lack thereof) shaped the opportunities you've had in comedy?

Ashley Nicole Black: When I first started out, I was doing the thing where I was like, trying not to be too employed so I could be very nimble in case a comedy job came up—which I think a lot of comedians do early on in their career. And for me that was actually very uncomfortable. I'm a person who needs stability and security and so I found that once I went ahead and accepted that promotion at work and was making a living wage, I was actually much more creative when I didn't have to worry about money all the time. So for me, [that meant] getting a day job. Having that made my security and just allowed me to be so much more free and creative.

What are some of the ways you had to sacrifice financially to get where you are today in comedy?

ANB: For me, personally, it wasn't necessarily about comedy, because I graduated into the recession—so I did have a lot of financial sacrifice but it wasn't because I chose comedy so much as because it was 2008. I had a series right after I left school

Photography courtesy of TBS

where every job I got, the company shut down a couple months after I started working there. So there was a lot of financial sacrifice. There was a time when I had to ask my parents to borrow money for my rent. I was walking places instead of taking cabs, or even the bus, and just really counting those pennies and trying to make them last until the end of the month. One thing you wouldn't [typically] consider a sacrifice . . . was that I wasn't paying my student loans, which means now that I'm a little bit more secure, I'm still dealing with the fallout from that period. But it wasn't comedy's fault. The recession just happened to happen around the time that I started in comedy.

In what ways can it be challenging for comedians to talk about the money they make before and after success?

ANB: I think before, it's actually pretty easy because (1), everybody's broke when they start out, and (2), comedians are known for being shameless and not having shame so I know when you're first starting out no one has a problem being like, "I'm broke, I can't afford to do that thing" or "No, obviously I'm not going on vacation, I'm a broke comedian." I think after success it actually gets harder to talk about money, because (1), you still have friends who are not there yet and you don't want to seem like you're bragging, and (2), so many factors of this business go into how much money people make; how many jobs you've had before, and even how talented your team is at negotiating. There are so many things that aren't about your skill or your talent that go into determining your pay—people can be wildly disparate and that can be really uncomfortable to

discuss because it can be for so many very subjective reasons.

Why do you think it's important for comedians to be more transparent about the money side of the job?

ANB: I think pay equity is the biggest thing. You know, some of the more well-qualified things have been like Mo'Nique finding out that she was offered so much less money by Netflix than other comics. The only way she could find that out is if she knew what those other comics were making. And so especially for those people who are at the top of their game who can (pun intended) afford to share that information, it can be helpful for the other people who are in more of the middle of their game to know what the goals are. But that is also very risky, I think. The people who have the most investment in pay equity are women and people of color because they are the people who are most likely to be underpaid. However, if the solution to pay equity is everyone sharing their pay, the people who have the most to lose by doing that are women and people of color. Because even though it was very clear that Mo'Nique was offered much less than she was worth, people got mad at her because it's sort of the norm to look at the situation and get mad at the most marginalized person. So it's a much bigger gamble for those people and they're the people who need it the most, so I see why it doesn't happen. Because if white men are being paid fairly then they have no reason to want to share their pay and to try to work on pay equity and pay transparency; the people who need the transparency and the equity may only be hurt by advocating for it.

What advice do you have for someone looking to make a decent living in comedy?

ANB: I think if it's about the money, you're not going to have a good time. If you're making comedy to make a living, you're going to be miserable because it's actually very hard to make a living making comedy. So for me, I always made sure I had a job that covered my basic needs. And then comedy was a means to express myself, a way to have fun with my friends. I love performing, it's the thing that makes me happiest in the world, if I made money from it, that was a cool, extra bonus. But I was in it to express myself and have fun with my friends and get that awesome rush of performing and speaking and being heard and making people laugh.

And if while you're doing that, the financial reward isn't coming, then my advice to people is always to just have another gig. And, yeah, that means maybe you're working longer hours than the next guy—and I remember when I was doing that sometimes I would get down because I would think, "Okay, I work forty hours a week and then I have to take those extra leftover hours and cram my comedy into them, where someone who doesn't have a full-time job has all of the hours of the week available to them to get better, and they're going to get better faster than me." But I was just determined that that wasn't going to be the case. And I stayed up nights and I forced myself to do it and I was like, "You know what, other people might have more opportunities or more money or whatever, but nobody is going to outwork me," and I just made that my motivation. **gc**

MARIA
BAMFORD

Interview by Natalie Pattillo
& Kelli Hart Kehler

*For comedian, actress, and voice actress
Maria Bamford, there's always an
opportunity to gain more understanding
of smart money practices (even attend-
ing 12-step groups about finances). But
when it comes to money and comedy—
and discerning who among your peers is
paid what—it's never uncomplicated.*

**How has financial stability (or lack
thereof) shaped the opportunities
you've had in comedy?**

Maria Bamford: In my experience, food and shelter insecurity aren't hilarious in real time. Maybe, once you have a sandwich and a safe place to live, you can have a few laughs. For me, lack of access to healthcare and being below the poverty line was rough. And I had to ask for a lot of help on how to have and keep a job. Even with every possible advantage as a white, college-educated lady from Minnesota, I needed a bunch of people—outside loving friends and family—to give me ideas and peer support on how to take care of the basic needs of one person. I went to support groups of all kinds: 12-step money groups, free therapy, library books, anything free.

I know having a secure family in childhood, childhood access to healthcare, and paid-for university education has helped raise my income, but I don't know all the statistics.

In what ways can it be challenging for comedians to talk about the money they make before and after success?

MB: I feel ashamed—like maybe I'm earning way more than my opening act, who is not only my professional peer, but a *friend*. That is uncomfortable and makes me feel like a creep. The way I've dealt with that was, for two years, I did profit sharing so that my friend and opening act received 30 percent of the net profit for each show. That was when the business had TV income and it was really fun. Now, I pay a guarantee of $1,200 plus air and hotel for every opener—unless it ends up short and I'm going to earn less than what they earn (but that hasn't happened yet!). The one thing that's permanent is showing every opener what my deal is and what I'm earning, so if they want to speak

up or ask questions, we both have all of the information available.

I think the part that is challenging is that *nobody* "deserves" an insane amount more pay than another. All work is important and I'd argue that the work the waitstaff is doing at a comedy club is much more important to people having a good time than what I'm doing. The reason I do well at my job is because of the work and efforts and infrastructure of thousands of people, and to the best of my ability, I want to make sure that everyone is acknowledged financially. I'm not perfect. I have forgotten cash to leave a tip for housekeeping service at a hotel—one of the hardest jobs you can have—but I try to always leave a $20 tip for each night.

How do you stay motivated/hustle when you're going through a financial rough patch?

MB: I go to 12-step groups for money. There are tons of them in L.A.—but they're also online and on the telephone. It's free. There can be a lot of Higher Power talk, but I just change that with cognitive behavioral science.

That's helped me feel less shame, in the good and the bad. I've been audited by the IRS five times, I've been close to homeless (didn't have the rent and a friend took me in without any money down), I've been out sick for a year, I've had collection agencies call and send threatening letters of "WE ARE NOW TAKING LEGAL ACTION!" The groups have given me the peace of mind that despite all appearances, there are no financial emergencies—if I can get food (I have gone to the food shelf) and shelter just for today, that's pretty good and maybe it's okay to have a good

day and a few laughs. Even if an IRS agent named Mr. Lopez is on my front doorstep asking to seize assets.

By the way, the IRS owed *me* $25, after all of that.

Do you think it's important for comedians to be more transparent about the money side of the job?

MB: No, I think it's whatever that is comfortable for you. It can help others—I think to better advocate for themselves if they know what the going rate is, but that doesn't guarantee that's what you'll get. There's still sexism, racism, ableism that's rampant in comedy. If you look at any lineup at every comedy club in the US, I would guess that 95 percent listed would be straight white males. I married a straight white male and he's super funny. If you look in L.A., at the clubs, most nights will have five guys and one woman up. It's odd. And it's real. There are anomalies and that's great, but I definitely think the only thing I can do (besides notice it) is to try to hire and share my business info with everybody. I've lucked out, for now, and I'm grateful to share if it's helpful. I'm also a comedian and I love attention and laughs and there is nothing more hilarious than someone who doesn't find me funny learning that I'm a multimillionaire because of comedy.

What advice do you have for someone looking to make a decent living in comedy?

MB: Do comedy. Do what you love, do what you find funny, make your own show (live in a theater or at a coffee shop or in your car) and do it again and again and again and again. Enjoy. 🐛

The Future Is Futuro

Stories about diversity and inclusion have entered America's mainstream discourse. But in its newsrooms, women of color are virtually absent. Emmy Award–winning journalist Maria Hinojosa is fighting for change at Futuro Media Group, one of the nation's only Latina-led nonprofit media organizations.

By Andrea Gompf
Photography by Melissa Bunni Elian

There was never any journalist who looked like me. So I really never thought, "I could do that." Later, I came to understand that invisibility, not seeing yourself present, actually has a psychological impact on you.

Born in Mexico and raised in Chicago, Maria Hinojosa doesn't recall ever seeing a journalist who looked like her when she was growing up. "When I found out what NPR was and who Susan Stamberg was, I remember thinking, 'Oh my god, what a cool job to be interviewing people every day. Wow,'" she shared with me on a recent afternoon in her Harlem apartment. "But I never thought, 'I could do that.' Never."

As it turned out, she could.

Over the last thirty years, Maria has built a trailblazing journalism career of firsts—among them, becoming the first Latina correspondent for both NPR and CNN. These experiences taught her the value of her underrepresented voice, and deepened her conviction to shine a light on other marginalized voices and perspectives. They also prepared her for one of her most important firsts yet: becoming the first Latina to found and lead an independent, nonprofit multimedia organization that centers communities long ignored by mainstream media.

The Futuro Media Group, which Maria founded in 2010, creates multiplatform cultural and political content for and by the diverse faces of America. Its media properties—which include Peabody Award–winning radio program Latino USA, political podcast In the Thick, digital news outlet Latino Rebels, and televised and digital documentary series—provide an essential alternative to commercial media outlets propelled by advertising dollars, ratings, or subscribers. Futuro's grant funding allows Hinojosa and her team of twenty-five to remain completely focused on their mission: to give a voice to the voiceless, and to counter harmful mainstream narratives that frame Latinos exclusively in the context of immigration and crime.

I spoke with Maria about her groundbreaking career, the process of founding and funding a nonprofit media project, and why spaces like Futuro are more critical than ever today.

What was your journey to becoming a journalist? I read your first taste was as host of a Latino radio show while you were a student at Barnard College.

My mom and my dad, all of us were born in Mexico. My dad was a medical doctor, [and became] a researcher at the University of Chicago. From the earliest time that I can remember, he always had *Time* magazine at his nightstand, he was always watching *Meet the Press*. That's what we did, we consumed news. But there was never any journalist who looked like me. The first Latino journalist I remember seeing on the air nationally was Geraldo. But Geraldo was Puerto Rican from New York, and that wasn't me. So I really never thought, "I could do that."

Later, I came to understand that invisibility, not seeing yourself present, actually has a psychological impact on you.

I originally came to New York because I wanted to be an actress. That's why I ended up at Barnard. The very first week of school I went to the Columbia University radio station, and the Latin American music department was very welcoming to me. Soon after that, I got my own radio show. It was the height of salsa in New York City, and the beginnings of hip-hop and rap. We were documenting all of that. And that's when I was like, "Oh, wait a second, this isn't just a little fun college thing, people are listening to my voice. And they're telling me that they appreciate that I'm putting these people on the air and interviewing them. Maybe I know what I'm doing here."

My last year of college, my career counselor basically forced me to apply for an internship at NPR. I got in and that changed everything. It was very strange, I was the very first Latina inside that editorial space. And then I was like, "Whoa, wait a second. How did this happen? I'm in here with this upper echelon of the most talented journalists. I don't really feel like I belong here, but I'm going to have to understand that I have a lot of privilege."

I was deeply insecure, as you can imagine, being the first one. And that's what forced me at a very young age to understand that

this privilege came with responsibility, so I needed to use my voice inside those newsrooms. That's how it started.

So much of your career has focused on shining a light on overlooked communities. Was there a formative moment when you realized that was your personal mission?

I tell this story, and the person it involves is actually a good friend of mine now, and one of my producers. He's a white guy, and it actually happened within the first month of my employment at NPR. The Mexico City earthquake had just happened, and there was also a plane that crashed taking off from Mexico City. My boss and I were coming back from an editorial meeting, and he was saying to me, "Wow, these two tragedies Mexico has just suffered through, the earthquake and now this plane crash. I don't know if the American people could handle two tragedies like this, one after another." Then he said, "I guess maybe Mexican people are used to it." And I remember this voice came out from my gut. I looked at him and I said, "Wait, no, what? No, no, no. People don't get used to this. You don't get used to suffering." I said this to my boss less than a month in.

I understood that my responsibility of privilege meant that I also had to speak truth when I saw it. He could have turned to me and said, "That was a little uppity of you to talk to your boss like that." Instead, what he said was, "Thank you for saying that. That was really important. It's like you're the conscience of this show."

I remember thinking, "Okay, this is what I have to do. I have to be honest."

That is something that really left a mark on me.

Before founding Futuro, your career in news and investigative journalism included working for both nonprofit institutions and commercial media. Was there anything in those experiences that steered you toward launching a nonprofit yourself?

I wanted to show that we can produce national journalism out of a community location. I wanted to show what it looks like when you have a consciousness of being representative when you're hiring.

I feel so lucky to have been able to have the experience of working in public media and also commercial media. My experience in public media allowed me to understand that there is a way of doing journalism that goes beyond breaking news. I understood that the journalism I was best at was going into communities, bringing these voices, hearing their perspective and putting them on a national platform. All of that is what I experienced in those early years at NPR, though it got harder and harder. Every year that went by, NPR was putting more and more pressure on its journalists to be more breaking news, more hard news, more short reporting.

Then CNN came calling and they said, "We want you to do longform." And I did that for about a year. And then CNN was bought by Time Warner, and then Fox News and there was all this pressure for ratings. When I went to CNN at first, they were letting me do five-and-a-half-minute pieces on the air. By the time I was leaving, they were looking at minute-by-minute ratings.

What did I learn when I was in mainstream commercial media? I learned that there are really good journalists who kick ass and that when you are a team of serious journalists you can do amazing work. But then I also learned what happens to a wonderful journalistic institution when

all of these values around making money, advertising dollars, holding eyeballs, start seeping in from the outside.

When you created Futuro, you expanded your role from journalist to CEO and executive producer. How did you go about making that shift, and what were some of the new skills you had to learn?

After my time at CNN, I worked on a show called *Now* on PBS that was independently produced. And that's what helped me to learn this other big career turn, which is seeing what it was to have a small production company. It was maybe thirty people, run by journalists who were now executive producing and running a company.

And there is a particular moment—I went in to tell my executive producer on the show [John Siceloff] that I wanted to be doing hour-long documentaries. And John said, "We want that for you too, Maria. We want you to have a big platform. So if you go raise the money, we'll do that."

I remember coming home and saying to my husband, "Honey, now I have to go raise my own money? What is this?" I was very upset. And then when I calmed down I was like, "Okay. I'm going to figure this out." And I actually did what a good journalist does. First, I found the issue that I

wanted to cover, then I found all kinds of sources, and then I asked those sources, "Look, I want to do this major documentary about child marriage. Do you know anyone who could support this?"

Boom. We raised money from Nike Foundation in a matter of a month.

That was my entry, and that's how it began to click. I was understanding that you have to ask for money. I'm from a Mexican family, immigrant family—we did not talk about money. You certainly didn't ask people for money. So first, I got real bold and I started asking.

And the thing that actually made me bold is the same thing that made me be bold in that NPR newsroom all those years ago. I was like, "Okay, so if I want to tell these stories, that means I've got to [get the courage] to ask the right foundations or philanthropists." It was the same thing in the NPR newsroom: "Okay, I'm terrified, I'm not sure what to do in this editorial meeting here with all these white folks, but I know I'm here for a reason. Raise your hand."

It's always been motivated by me wanting to put these stories out there.

What made you decide to start Futuro in 2010?

Now on PBS got canceled and I was at a point in my life thinking, "What am I going to do?" Then something clicked, and I thought, "I know a lot of Hollywood actresses have formed their own production companies. I've seen them doing it." I didn't know any woman journalist that had formed her own production company to do news. But the economic downturn had happened, and journalists were losing their jobs. People were trying to figure out how to do things on their own.

How did you get the company off the ground?

Let's go back to 9/11, which is a big marker in my life for all kinds of reasons. One of the things that happened after 9/11, is that I developed PTSD. [My treatment] led me to an acupuncturist, who recommended I begin working with a healer named Fiona [Druckenmiller]. I go in, and a small blond-haired woman right around my age does a kind of Reiki on me. I had never done anything like that and it was really special. She became my healer. I was speaking with her about very intimate things. But the thing about Fiona was that she didn't charge. And in New York everybody charges, so I was intrigued. Long story short, I did a lot of research and figured out that Fiona was actually a multimillionaire, from one of the richest families in the United States of America.

That was in 2001. Now, it's 2007 and I'm learning how to raise money. I find out Fiona has given money to journalists, [so

I ask her] "Fiona, would you help support my documentary on women in power in politics? I want to go to Rwanda." And she said, "Okay!" She was my healer, she loved me. I loved her.

So then all of a sudden when I was in this [career] moment where I'm like, "What the hell am I going to do?" I asked to meet with Fiona. I said, "Will you help me? Angel investors invest in women at 1 percent, but invest in men 99 percent. I'm going to do Futuro as a nonprofit, this is not about making money."

Fiona gave us the first grant, and I think our second grant was the Marguerite Casey Foundation. Now, the Ford Foundation is our major funder. We are in existence because of Fiona and because of Ford. That's how it all started.

Can you walk me through some of the nitty-gritty of fund-raising and creating a nonprofit?

In the beginning I tapped into my network. I talked to my friends and people who I know about running a nonprofit. I had conversations with them about their own nonprofits. I asked a lot of questions.

I really did not know how to do this, so I had a business partner at first. He helped me to set up the 501(c)(3), to have a sense of the basic things, like establishing bylaws. But within the first year, we realized we had very different visions and it didn't work out. The lesson there is anything

can happen. And it's going to feel like an earthquake, but you're still alive so you just have to breathe through it.

Rossana Rosado, who is the New York secretary of state right now, and who is a friend, always said to me, "People are going to want to support a person who has a sense of mission. So if you don't have the exact business-plan layout, paperwork, all that—you'll find out how to do that. First, you have to have that passion. That's the thing that's going to unlock the money."

I definitely have the passion. If people believe in your mission, they will give.

Do you think the role of Futuro has changed in these last two years, given our political context?

When I formed Futuro, I was very clear. In 2010, the census had come out and one of the numbers that stuck with me was 43 percent, which was the Latino demographic growth from 2000 to 2010. This data is hard data. I understood then what people now call "the new mainstream." I was doing radio journalism, and everybody except for Fiona was like, "Okay, Maria, you're going to start a company that's basically got one radio product, radio is dying, and you want to talk about race and diversity at a time when people are getting along. We don't really get it." Now here we are eight years later and it's clear that we were right to be talking about data, we were right to be talking about demographics, we were right to be talking about honest representation.

Latino USA's audience has grown by 50 percent over the last five years. People want to know about Latinos and Latinas. Did I think that was where my career was going to be right now? No. But it's exactly where it needs to be, because, my gosh, Latinos and Latinas and immigrants are the most attacked group right now in the United States of America, apart from Black men, who are being murdered indiscriminately.

Our journalistic core is to be truthful, to be honest, and to give context for what's happening as Latinos and Latinas, the most targeted group hated by this president. So we are all together understanding how is our role shifting.

What's next for Futuro?

I wanted to show that we can produce national journalism out of a community location. And we've done that. And I wanted to show what it looks like when you have a consciousness of being representative when you're hiring. My company is run by an African American woman and I'm a Mexican woman. My chair of the board is a woman of Indian descent.

Journalistically, we're doing great, we won the Peabody, we won the Robert F. Kennedy Award with our investigations, and we're doing more investigative work. We're experimenting with growing that part of the company, solid journalism, narrative journalism, more podcasts. And not giving up our foot in the world of television. We're thinking about what we could do

that is commercial and able to sit with our ethos, with our mission. And I think what we want to do is use the stories that we're gathering for the basis of dramatic work, episodic on Hulu or Netflix or feature film, based on real-life stories. The people we meet are just fascinating, and we own the life rights to a couple of their stories.

What would you like to see change in terms of the landscape of funding for POC-centered journalism?

So many people say to me, "Why did you make [Futuro] a nonprofit?" And what people don't understand is one of the things that has damaged American journalism is the commercialization and the business of American journalism. A network recently told me, "Look, immigration reporting doesn't deliver on the ratings." I was horrified. So that's why we need to have journalism that is not tied to what the ratings are.

I don't have the answer. Certainly, the Corporation for Public Broadcasting is not the answer. But I think you have to have robust philanthropic support, because if we are constantly looking at the bottom line, we're always going to be faced with challenges. What we need is a massive fund that is independently run to support media that is independent. And it could even support commercial media, if they really delivered on the things that they promise.

And it's not just about funding journalism, it's actually funding journalistic institutions that are run by POC, that are run by people who are actively saying, "We are part of the tradition of American journalism. You need to see us."

What if we had started funding [POC-led] institutions to cover our demographic in 2001? Would Trump have been able to win if we had been massively telling the true story of immigrants and immigration? We're not here to replace you. We want to come to work with you, fall in love with you, hang out with you, be your neighbors. **gc**

20 MAJOR lessons

LEARNED ABOUT $MONEY AS a FREELANCE illustrator

full time

BY ANDREA PIPPINS

A visual essay highlighting some tips, reflections, journal musings, and annoyances I've collected during the first few years of my career as an entrepreneur and freelance illustrator.

1. Over the years I've learned to negotiate and always ask for more.

2. I make sure every client signs a contract because I have been burned before.

3. Quitting my day job was necessary for me, but a financial struggle at first. I wish I had more of a cushion for slow times in those early days.

4. Unlike a salary, money doesn't always come on time. I'm learning to prepare for those days.

5. I've connected my self-worth to how much money is in my bank account—which is terrible. My finances have nothing to do with who I am.

6. Money attracts money, so I try to keep my bank balance at a certain amount to attract more.

7. Money is an exchange for my skills, service, and time, so I appreciate every single penny that I've earned.

8. Creating an invoicing system helps me manage who owes me what and when.

9. May sound obvious but opening a business bank account really helped me manage my money. Especially for taxes.

10. Creating a positive money mantra that I say, think, and write every day helps me manifest more opportunities to call in more money.

11 This was and is one of the biggest lessons I've learned: working hard or working more does not always equal more money. It's the world's biggest myth. So I've been figuring out ways to work less but make more.

12. One way I've learned to work less is by having multiple streams of income, including a few sources of passive income.

13. Don't be afraid to talk to fellow freelancers about money. I love getting different perspectives.

14. Hiring a good accountant keeps my money managing tight – especially for taxes.

15. Reading and listening to interviews with money experts helps me stay educated about finances. (Honestly, I need to do more of this.)

16. I've learned that money comes in cycles, sometimes a lot all at once and then nothing. So I prepare for those rainy days.

17. I'm now making big money goals, which means dreaming a lot bigger.

18. Lately, I've been focusing on saying yes to the opportunity first, and then thinking about the money. That way I'm not doing the work just for the money.

19. Setting aside money for taxes gives me peace of mind.

20. I grew up hearing a lot of negative talk about money. I'm working on changing that script and creating a new, more abundant narrative for myself.

When Purpose Meets Business

From tech to fashion, these founders commit their work to social impact.

By Anna Watt
Photo collage by Katy Edling

When a business idea is driven by purpose and desire to make an impact, the results can be so much more rewarding than just a paycheck. From building technology as a platform for social good to creating an ethical fashion label, these entrepreneurs raise the voices of their audience and provide invaluable resources to their communities.

Kortney Ziegler and Tiffany Mikell of ZaMLabs created Appolition, an app that converts spare change to bail money for people who are incarcerated, because they were inspired by the work grassroots organizations were doing in rallying people to contribute to community bail funds.

"The main challenge for us was to find a partner willing to trust our lead and expertise as technologists in helping to bolster the work they were already doing organically. We discovered that National Bail Out—a collective of organizations fighting mass incarceration—were the best people to be our inaugural partner, as they had already done great work in spotlighting communities coming together to pay bail for others," Kortney said of the unique challenges of starting a business with a cause at its core.

Whitney Manney, artist and founder of WHITNEYMANNEY, an independent fashion and textile label that is "ethical, not boring," is building a culture of challenging women to wear their statement.

"I saw the opportunity to create a visual statement for myself when it felt like having a say in defining myself was impossible," said Whitney. "The older I got, the more I realized I couldn't be alone in those feelings, especially as a Black girl who doesn't fit

"Being able to make something that is adopted by thousands, with the goal of helping others, is deeply rewarding and humbling at the same time." –Kortney Ziegler

the 'traditional' mold. Developing a brand that combined building self-confidence and cultural significance, plus smashing fine-art fiber processes into an accessible ready-to-wear format, was something to work through. I was definitely questioned, challenged, and doubted. We should be able to make a statement through fashion and it doesn't have to be a couture gown. I want to be able to wear my confidence on my sleeve every day."

As with running any business, there's always the bottom line (that's business speak for making money). Companies still have to keep the lights on and pay the bills, but there's something so authentic and inspiring when a business can make decisions that keep people, products, and purpose all in mind, and still be successful.

"We believe that you can make a tech product that is engaging and useful for users and be economically sustainable if you do focus on team-building and creating a great experience for users," said Kortney, who has successfully cofounded multiple start-ups and a nonprofit.

Kortney and his cofounder, Tiffany, self-funded their platform. Now they are raising seed money to keep up with growth and demand. "So many people are excited to know they can do something that seems so small, like donating pocket change, but make a significant impact at the same time," said Kortney.

Whitney, who has been building her business since college, is driven by the idea of making something out of nothing. "Creating work with my own textiles has always been important to me, as well as working with sustainable fabrics. Sometimes I've had grand ideas for a design but come right back to reality when I crunched the numbers for fabric cost. You always have to compromise and problem solve," said Whitney.

Whitney, who says her work can be time-consuming since many pieces are custom-made from hand-dyed or digitally printed fabric, had to devise solutions that would allow her business to still be profitable but also accessible to her customers.

"I had to quickly come up with ideas that can float the business in between those custom orders," said Whitney. "Being able to put my textile designs on small goods like accessories, home decor, et cetera, allows me to have consistent 'bread and butter.' Knowing which products will or won't be a hit is a never-ending equation, but it allows me to outsource, refresh creatively, and develop new work that is important to me. My goal is to never dilute the value and message of the brand but I want those who admire my work to be a part of the world of WHITNEYMANNEY."

Creating a business for purpose beyond profit can also be a personally rewarding experience. Kortney says he is excited about the opportunity to now operate in the tech space because of the infinite applications of code and other digital tools that are available to create change. "Being able to make something that is adopted by thousands, with the goal of helping others, is deeply rewarding and humbling at the same time," said Kortney.

For Whitney, being successful means giving it her all in the studio, but she also saves some of her energy and talent for her community. "Through teaching workshops in the community, I'm able to work with a lot of girls who are the age I was when I decided to teach myself how to sew," said Whitney. "As they learn how to work a machine, complete first projects, and have conversations with me about their future, I am reminded why I am here and why I need to keep moving forward."

If the meaningful and positive impact has sparked inspiration for your own social-good business, Kortney says the first step is figuring out what problem you're solving. "Once you do that, talking to people that might want to support as a user or customer will help guide the way in which you solve for that problem," said Kortney.

Whitney offered the advice that being aware, reflecting, and building that confidence to really define your priorities is crucial. "You are going to be consistently asked and pushed about your 'why,'" said Whitney. "You have to make sure you are unwavering. Trust that what is captivating about your story will come naturally; people can immediately tell when you're trying to force anything. Have a crew or mentor that can help you during those hard times. It will surprise you where support for your business does or does not come from. Remember that all of this is bigger than you, and find ways to consistently give back." gc

Want *More* Good Company?

Every week, Good Company's editor in chief,
Grace Bonney, talks with some of the most inspiring and
innovative creative entrepreneurs about life and work.

Each episode provides motivation, inspiration,
practical advice, and a vital sense of connection and
community for creatives at every stage of life.
Every episode of Good Company is focused on honest, open
conversations about the ups and downs of creative life.

For more information, visit welcometogoodcompany.com/podcast

Subscribe and listen to the Good Company podcast on
iTunes, Stitcher, Simplecast, Google Play & Spotify.

How to Know Your Worth: Gearing Up and Going After It

The importance of standing your ground—and raising your voice—to get what you deserve.

By Caroline Choe
Illustration by Marly Gallardo

I still remember the first time I asked for a raise. I was twenty-two years old and had been working at a day camp for four summers, since I'd turned eighteen. I was always told I was a hard worker, responsible, and was even asked to substitute for my supervisor when she was sick. Every summer offered up the chance to earn some money, which definitely helped in the first semester of college, and at that point I was a recent college graduate trying to build my own life.

My young male colleagues at the time who had asked for a raise were granted one, all with different years in experience working at the camp and for all the various reasons that were theirs. One would think I had a great setup for the case I would present.

But, no, it was a degrading conversation where I was told by the director in a condescending little-girl-you-listen-to-me tone that I would "make more money in tips," and with a blistered cherry on top, he added: "You'll thank me one day."

I wish I could say this was the last time I would encounter this in my life, but indeed it was just the beginning.

Say what you think you're worth, and don't be afraid to put the number on the table. If the person next to you wasn't afraid to say it, neither should you.

The Piano Finally Hit My Head.

Soon after that happened, I began what would be fourteen years of a professional teaching career. It would span several schools, going from assisting to eventually leading in classrooms, achieving my master's degree in art education, and moving on to what I'd hoped were bigger opportunities and, truthfully, a bigger paycheck in doing the job I loved to do.

Though I did find other work, little by little, the veil was coming off in my adulthood. Despite the fact that I was making more than some of my male friends in the very first moments of my career, eventually I would come to realize that they were receiving larger paychecks in shorter time. Sure enough, nearly every time, they were granted these requests, and by both male and female directors. According to their shared accounts, they also didn't have to think about negotiating as strategically or carefully. Later on, I would also consistently observe there being more financial mercy and job acceleration being reserved especially for my white coworkers, despite my credentials and years of experience.

If I asked questions, I was considered difficult, whiny, a squeaky wheel to the equation that ultimately worked for those it was asked to. Many times, my motives were questioned and the terms would boil down to things needing to be "conditional," also known as doing more work than what was originally asked.

The only times I'd ever gotten any possibilities to negotiate a salary raise was whenever my director was a woman. I had to wonder if this was going to continue on throughout my life, if the only people who could see the reasoning in what I was asking would be fellow women.

However, this still didn't excuse the guilt or apprehension I had whenever I'd felt the nudge of needing to ask for more. If the offer was so sweet, why didn't I feel right about it? This couldn't be something I was afraid of bringing up just to avoid an uncomfortable conversation. The situation could always go one of two ways: They could say yes or no. Whatever direction it pointed to, I could make my next choices based on it. If someone or a place wouldn't help me grow, then I just had to keep moving until I found a place that would. I needed to approach each situation as my biggest advocate and not be afraid to push, despite the fact that in many cases I got so physically, emotionally, and mentally tired of this fight. In the end, this was something that wasn't just happening to me.

If I ultimately knew and owned the value in the work that I did and knew what I wanted, this would always serve as the fuel for the change I wanted in my life.

It's Time.

The best advice I ever received in both my careers was simply put: Say what you think you're worth, and don't be afraid to put the number on the table. If the person next to you wasn't afraid to say it, neither should you.

After being a teacher for over a decade, I made the decision to establish a small business that would be my passion project to work exclusively in food and the arts. I wanted every day to proactively teach, make, and advocate for the causes that I knew had the universal abilities to bridge and translate over any differences between people. Along the way, I came to a few revelations in my beginnings. I would need to start from the bottom again, providing some free services here and there until that well went dry. Now nearly two handfuls of years later, I know to speak up when my BS radar goes off, with plenty of people looking for freebies. Experience is great, but we all have to eat and pay the bills. I had to learn to put my foot down, acknowledge the position I'd earned, and also be willing to be slow on bill paying some months. However, it was what was needed so I wouldn't constantly shortchange myself to someone else's financial comfort level. There were plenty of instances when event planners wanted free services for their event in exchange for "free advertising," "exposure," and "connections." In some cases, you get promised a free meal with your time, or other things that could lead to building a great potential new professional relationship. After a while, with some you'll see more clearly that the only connection you made was that they got to have several big events and not pay their vendors properly for whatever was provided. Though I was grateful to learn and do the work, I still needed more than what they were offering. If I wasn't saying it, my accountant definitely did at the end of my first year of business.

Despite the setbacks one might encounter and the headaches you can endure, you will indeed find the people who will say yes to what you're asking for. If you say to them that this is the only factor that is holding you back from working with them, whatever happens next will be a telling move. I did finally find schools that were willing to negotiate a higher yearly salary, and I did find people who were interested in the lessons and services I provided. However these moments ended up panning out, I remember them mostly by how they were handled. For some, the wage raise itself might be the strongest factor, but for me, it's what remained more meaningful on top of it. Throughout every experience, no matter how big or brittle, self-respect is the one thing I have to hold as high as the money itself. I think that's the only way I've ever been fulfilled by any of it.

Throughout all of this, the best thing I could say that came is what I felt was leaving behind a better starting block for the person who eventually would fulfill that role. If we want a better future not only for ourselves but also for others, we have to not be afraid to take that stand.

Though things have gotten better, I can't say the coin has completely flipped itself yet. I still do run my own business, but like many, I constantly face the stigma of what my services are worth compared to what's available in the bigger-scale market. Yet I can't apologize for standing my ground in this consistently uncomfortable topic. I can't wait for someone to fight for me, but I can hope that I'll be able to hold it all down until someone just might.

Within all this experience, it gave me the chance to form and practice personal and professional mantras:

- In the end, if you don't ask the question, you don't get an answer. You say how much your work is worth, and get to decide when "the end" is.

- Go in and say what you want, and it's both your jobs to deliver what's promised.

- If you don't fight for something, they'll never know how much you want it.

- Hopefully one day soon, we won't always have to fight for it.

The challenge will almost always present itself, so when you're asked to perform a job or lend your services, communicate your asking price or ask if a higher fee than what they presented can be negotiated. If you're presented with pushback, stand strong and be ready to offer up your reasons. You'll have a checklist of background facts to include why your fee is this rate or what the industry standards are. If after all that it's not enough to convince them, be mentally prepared to walk away from the offer; allow yourself to be disappointed, but let it be just a stepping stone.

As women, we have taken the time at hand and seized it. I hope that we continue on this streak where realization of self-worth just becomes innate knowledge.

There have been a few times after that first time when I have walked away livid from such moments, but I didn't have then the voice I have now. There's much I still don't know about what will happen in the future, but what I do know is that it is going to continue being used, with or without permission. gc

Sometimes the Most Meaningful Pay Isn't Monetary

One hospice volunteer shares the universal life lessons she learned in caring for the dying.

By Lindsay Curtis
Photography by Hannah Yoon

When I began volunteering with hospice as a Reiki volunteer, I saw it as a way to pay forward the kindness and compassion that was given to me and my family many years earlier when I was a child and my dad was dying of cancer. As a volunteer, I was prepared to give of myself and my time without expecting anything in return. What I didn't yet know—but would soon learn—was the great extent to which my patients and their families would enrich my life when they opened their homes and hearts to me.

In working with the dying, I've been inspired by the depths of human resilience in the face of pain and uncertainty. I've learned that we often get caught up in the details of our busy lives, focusing on acquiring material things instead of what truly matters: our connections with other people. Above all, I witnessed over and over again that the most transformative and meaningful thing we can offer to anyone—no matter our race, culture, creed, or socioeconomic status—is our presence and love.

My Saturday morning routine was simple. Wake up. Shower. Have some coffee. Hop on my rusty bike and—rain or shine—cycle through downtown Toronto, navigating the streets of the new-to-me city to make my way to Laila's condo. Once there, I'd check in with the doorman in the lobby of her posh building before making my way up to her fifty-second-floor penthouse. Stepping into the condo with floor-to-ceiling windows and a breathtaking view of Lake Ontario was always a bit surreal—a far cry from my one-bedroom basement apartment with a single window placed in the outdated bathroom. Despite the differences in our ways of living, a sense of peace would always wash over me as I would pad my way into Laila's bedroom, where she lay waiting for me.

Laila was dying, and I was there as a hospice palliative-care volunteer to give her Reiki, a form of energy healing that can be used for anything from stress reduction to pain relief and relaxation. At fifty-two years old, Laila was diagnosed with ovarian cancer. After exhausting all of the treatment options available to her, she received the news: Nothing more could be done. She and her husband turned to hospice to provide her with care in her final weeks, and that is when our paths crossed.

At each of our Saturday morning visits, it became clear that my time with Laila was about so much more than Reiki. Perhaps because I wasn't a family member or friend, she felt safe sharing some of her most vulnerable thoughts with me: memories about her life's joys and regrets as well as her feelings and fears about her impending death. As the weeks carried on and Laila's body shrunk, her desire to live a heart-led life grew. She wanted to give as much as she could to others in the short time she had left earthside.

On the day of our last visit, the weather matched my mood, and it poured with rain on my bike ride to Laila's home. After our usual Reiki treatment, we exchanged cards and cried as we hugged each other—our final goodbye. As a way of thanking me for the time I'd spent with her, Laila wanted to gift me a necklace that had been in her family for generations. Because of the intimate nature of the work, hospice workers and clients can sometimes lose sight of the fine line between being a friend and

being a member of their caregiving team. Thanks to my training, I knew that being compensated as a hospice volunteer—even with gifts from the clients we cared for—was strictly forbidden.

Because our time together was always meant to be about and for Laila, I did not talk about myself much during our visits. But in this final goodbye, Laila wanted to know: Why would a young woman like me want to volunteer for hospice?

At just three and six years of age, my little sister and I knew very little about what was happening to our dad, to us, to our family. We only knew that our father, who was only twenty-six years old and recently diagnosed with cancer, was very sick. When a hospital bed and other medical equipment were brought into our home in our dad's final days, we were instructed to be quiet and careful around him. Thanks to the kindness of one hospice nurse, one of the strongest memories I have from my childhood involves cuddling my frail father as he lay in the bed placed in the middle of our living room. I distinctly remember watching the nurse's eyes fill with tears after she helped me and my sister up into his bed to snuggle him. She must have known what we couldn't have—that my dad was only days away from death.

The gift that the nurse gave me in allowing me to cuddle my father left an indelible mark on my heart and soul. Long after my dad passed away, my mom would sing the praises of the hospice staff and the profound impact they had on her life. They gave her strength when she felt she had none; support when her life was falling apart. They even gave her hope that she would be okay as a young widow with two small children. So when I saw an online ad calling for hospice volunteers within a

month of arriving in my new city, I knew it was my chance to use my time and skills as a way of paying forward the kindness that had been offered to our family by hospice staff many years earlier.

The hospice volunteer training was an intensive fifty hours over the course of a month. It prepared me for how to conduct myself and how to talk with the dying, but it did not prepare me for the fact that although I was getting no monetary compensation, I would be paid in dividends in universal life lessons learned at the bedside of the clients I cared for. I've adopted some of the values and attitudes that dying patients embrace, and it has helped me live a heart-centered life.

Give of yourself by being of service to others. You never know whose life you might change for the better—yours included.

No matter our life story, most of us share the same sentiments at the end of life: to love more and to follow our own dreams.

I've seen clients with various spiritual beliefs, unique family structures, and diverse ways of life. Although each client's individual story was different, there were overwhelming similarities among all of them. When our own mortality is in front of us, we all wish to right any wrongs we feel we've done in our lives. We strive to live a heart-centered life in the time we have left. We want to share love and make meaningful connections with others.

One of my youngest clients, Dean, was a father of four small children. Like many others, Dean expressed regret in not pursuing his own dreams, but rather the dreams other people had for him. Through Dean, I learned the importance of following your own passion rather than doing what others think you should do.

Our shared humanity connects us all.

On the surface, it would seem as if Laila and I had almost nothing in common. I was gay and single, she was straight and married. I was broke, she was wealthy. I was still in school, she had many degrees. But despite our differences on the surface, we found ways to connect in our shared humanity. All of us have similar needs and desires as humans—the need to feel and give love, the need to belong, the need to make a positive impact on the world around us.

Every person we encounter has a story to share and something to teach us. We are more alike than we are different. Knowing this has helped me make deep and meaningful connections with others, no matter our differences, and has encouraged me to extend kindness and grace to others during life's difficult moments.

When words fail us, sometimes the most impactful thing we can do is just be present.

Being a compassionate presence is a skill that's not often heralded in our fast-paced, chatterbox world. One of the most precious gifts we can offer to someone is not advice. Not material things. Just our presence. When we're bogged down in the busyness of our daily routines, it's easy to forget to be present with the people around us. Sitting in companionable silence is a lovely, intimate experience that we should all make more time for.

The daily minutiae, the drama, the "stuff" we accumulate—none of it really matters.

What does matter is our relationships with other people, enjoying life experiences, and pursuing the things that make us happy. No one reaches the end of their life wishing they'd spent more time at work, but they do often express a desire to spend more time with loved ones. We can enrich our relationships by saying "I love you" more often, by listening and truly hearing what others have to say. Embrace the world—and the people—around you as much as you can.

We can find joy (almost) anywhere.

Perhaps surprisingly, most of the conversations I've had with hospice clients were not centered around death. Most of us, even when we are dying, want to talk about life. We want to connect with others by sharing happy memories, laughter, and love. Even in our darkest times, we are reaching for hope and happiness. The dying have taught me that it is important to embrace moments of joy as they come.

The most common responses I hear from people after I've told them I've been a hospice volunteer include "Oh, I could never do that" and "That sounds so depressing." Both statements are usually accompanied by a look of pity. But it's the contrary—volunteering for hospice has enriched my life beyond measure.

Although I have never been financially compensated for my hospice work, I have earned things much more valuable than money. My community has grown through connections with fellow volunteers. I've been paid in spades through the wisdom those at the end of their lives have shared with me. Material things don't matter at the end of life (or even in the middle of it). Don't wait until your health fails to live the life you want. Love fully. You can settle, or you can create a life full of passion, meaning, and fulfillment. The choice is yours. Give of yourself by being of service to others. You never know whose life you might change for the better—yours included. **gc**

Note from the editor: The names of the patients in this story have been changed to protect their identities and medical histories.

Paying Your Bills with Podcasts

How five podcasters are (slowly, maybe, hopefully) making a living in audio.

By Amanda McLoughlin
Photo collage by Francisca Pageo

I'm going to tell you something that I was so worried to tell my parents: I quit my job to become a full-time podcaster. After three years of making shows at night, over lunch breaks, and on weekends, I took the plunge and committed to my dream.

It's an uncertain time to be taking this risk (not that there is ever a good time to quit your job to make art). Search for "podcast" in the news and you'll find an avalanche of articles foretelling the future of the audio industry. Some say it's booming, with advertising dollars pouring in

and companies announcing new shows by the dozen. Others point to high-profile layoffs as an early warning sign that this once-special medium is on its way out.

Despite the uncertainty, thousands of podcasters are building communities around their shows every day. Some of the most rule-breaking, genre-bending work being done today is in audio. But artistic merit doesn't always equal commercial success. Unless you're reaching tens of thousands of people with your show, you have to rely on donations, crowdfunding, work for hire, and/or unconventional sponsorship

arrangements with small businesses. I lean on all four to pay my rent each month. Making a living as a podcaster feels like a magic trick that I don't really know how to do, even as I'm doing it.

Just because a podcast is popular doesn't mean it's profitable. One of the biggest names in podcasting right now is Cameron Esposito, host of *Queery* and *Put Your Hands Together*. Esposito is also a writer, actor, and producer who views podcasting as "a side gig I am very passionate about. **There is a lot of freedom in not relying on podcasting as a single or**

> *"A rising tide lifts all boats, so we always share our day rates and salary information with each other. If they make more money, we all make more money, simple as that." –James T. Green*

major source of income, and for almost all podcasters, this is the setup. Very few of us make enough to be able to focus solely on podcasting." She calls both of her shows **"labors of love"** that "mostly afford me artistic expression and a chance to build, and connect with, the queer and comedy communities (and the overlap thereof). Because neither is a major source of income, I plan their recording and distribution around the other commitments and goals I have in my work life." Esposito relies on ad revenue from *Queery* to compensate the show's producer and "the support of a major podcast network for audio engineering, ad sales, and many other behind-the-scenes parts of podcasts. We both win: They get content and I get support."

Jeffrey Masters, host of the show *LGBTQ&A*, says that podcasting makes up less than 5 percent of his income. "[The show is] now two years old, and last month I received my first check from ad sales. It was for $120," he says. His show rewards him in other ways, though. "I've leveraged my podcast to get paid to write for many publications that I admire, and have gotten paid to speak at universities, film festivals, and many other events. I've been able to meet an incredible number of industry leaders, as well as my personal heroes. Those **connections** have been really valuable professionally, and many of these people have also become friends, which has added a great deal of richness to my life." Jeffrey's point hit home for me. Podcasters are incredibly generous and creative people as a rule, and I'm lucky to count many among my friends. Creative projects don't need to be profitable to be worth doing. But what do we do when we need to choose between making money at a day job and making art?

Debbie Millman, host of the fourteen-years-old-and-counting podcast *Design Matters*, initially saw money as a corrupting influence on her work. She was working primarily in the corporate world and felt that her creative spirit was slipping away. "For most of my trajectory as a podcaster, I was adamant about **keeping the podcast 'pure'** and not taking any type of advertising," she says. But when she and her colleagues decided to create a new print magazine, she realized she could fund the entire production of the publication by accepting advertisers onto her show. Once there was an artistically motivated reason to open up the show to advertising, Millman started to build ethical and sustainable sponsor relationships. "I am working with just a few advertisers that have become season sponsors of the show, so there is a real partnership that is being developed," she says. *Design Matters* also participates in Drip, a new crowdsourcing funding platform by Kickstarter. Like Esposito, Millman can afford to reinvest her podcast's revenue into her art since she has other forms of income as a teacher, writer, speaker, and president of a consulting business.

For many podcasters, the ideal intersection of art and commerce is a full-time salaried job with benefits making an excellent show. As a producer at the Radiotopia banner show *99% Invisible*, Avery Trufelman has one of those jobs—but her path there was meandering and full of unpaid work. "I started out interning at Air America and WNYC in the summers between school, which were unpaid and once a week," she says. "I would work in restaurants on the other days. When I started applying to full-time jobs, I was put through the ringer and roundly rejected from every job I applied to. And after a stint interning for *Latino USA* (also unpaid), I heard about an internship with *99% Invisible*, one of my favorite podcasts. I figured it would be my last shot: If I couldn't get the job, clearly this wasn't the career path for me. And then I got it!" Trufelman points to her parents, both of whom have worked at public radio station WNYC, as living examples of people who made art for a living and still managed to keep a roof over their heads. Without that example, Trufelman doesn't know if she would have known it was possible to make it in her chosen career.

Freelance producer James T. Green also credits a full-time job with benefits as a crucial step in his podcastng career. He grew to love podcasts through shows like *The Black Guy Who Tips* while working in tech, and started learning how to make audio through free online tutorials while working a full-time position. Soon, he wanted to make a show of his own, and "teamed up with some friends in the Chicago creative community to create Postloudness, a collective of independent audio shows hosted by people of color, women, and queer-identified hosts." He eventually got a job in audio with MTV, which helped relocate him to New York City. His next few jobs taught him a lot, but not all came with benefits. "I did a flurry of freelance gigs, hopping on as showrunner for pilots that went nowhere, consulting for shows, engineering quick projects, editing other people's stories, and pitching my own," he says. "Bills were getting paid, but things were tough, and **a partner that had a steady job and benefits** was helpful."

Each of these conversations felt like a sigh of relief as I finally got to talk with fellow podcasters about the difficult financial realities of this medium. Most of us, including my interview subjects, **don't talk about money** with fellow podcasters. This was the first time that Millman, Esposito, and Masters had discussed money and podcasting. Trufelman used to talk about money more openly, since there was less of it to go around before *Serial* set off a podcasting boom by breaking into the mainstream cultural conversation in the US. Once advertisers, legacy media companies, and corporations got interested in podcasting, it became possible to make a lot of money in this medium. Before big money started pouring in, "there was this assumption that we were all pretty much scraping by," Trufelman says; now, with a growing wealth disparity among podcasters, it feels gauche to talk about income. But as a freelance producer in charge of negotiating his own compensation, Green discusses money often. He says that this is especially true "with women and non-binary folks in

podcasting who are sadly still hit with lesser pay." He believes that "**a rising tide lifts all boats**, so we always share our day rates and salary information with each other. If they make more money, we all make more money, simple as that."

I cornered my interview subjects in the first place so I could find out how other people made a living in this industry. We had great discussions about money and art, but I needed some advice. So I asked what each of them would say to fellow podcasters trying to break into the medium. Green says, "Negotiate your contracts: Ask to retain the intellectual property of your creations, and try to work on a nonexclusive basis so you can try other projects simultaneously. And always remember not to lose your identity to the company you work at. Your reputation is everything." He also finds it useful to "have a **layoff fund** that you shuttle away any time you have cash coming in (shout-out to Gaby Del Valle!). Full-time jobs are **not necessarily secure**—there's always a chance you can be laid off."

Millman echoes that sentiment, reminding fellow creatives to "always, always, always **live below your means**. Save as much money as you can. Contribute the maximum to your 401(k) if you have a day job, or an IRA if you are self-employed. Pay your taxes on time. Don't get into credit card debt; pay your full balance every month. And make sure you have a good financial consultant!" Looking back over her career, she wishes she realized earlier that "**money might make things easier**, but it will not change who you are deep down inside."

Masters and Trufelman agreed that newcomers to podcasting should not expect to make money right away. "Don't ignore nonfinancial perks," Masters suggests. "Celebrate small wins, and **don't be afraid to talk yourself up**. If you don't believe in yourself, why would someone that you don't know believe in you?" Trufelman adds, "There's a lot of advice out there about making sure you know your worth, and that's absolutely true. Listening to someone's drafts (who is not a friend) or giving a talk (at a place that is not a charity) are labor and **should be compensated** with at least a small honorarium."

Esposito sees similarities between podcasting and touring as a stand-up comic. "I started doing stand-up by cobbling a living together from a bunch of varied sources—live performance, teaching, hosting corporate gigs. I wish I knew that it was never going to be different than that—the arts and entertainment industries demand **a small-business person's hustle** and an ability to pivot and always seek out new income sources to keep yourself afloat."

There is no one route to financial stability or commercial success in podcasting. But there's also no ceiling to what the passionate, inventive, relentless artists working in this form can achieve. We might all be making it up as we go along, but we're also redefining success for ourselves every day. As I embark on this exhilarating journey of full-time podcasting, I am going to keep in mind Esposito's final word of advice: "A lifelong creative career will survive many, many failures." **gc**

$7.82 NO HEALTH INSURANCE

RDU → ABQ
$325 SEE
BEST FRIEND

$4.12 MOUSE TRAPS (12)

CANDY
$1.26 AT GAS STATION

emotionally
SPENT

WHAT WE BUY AND HOW WE FEEL ABOUT IT

BY IRIS GOTTLIEB

$1,821 NEW WATER HEATER; NO HOT WATER FOR 6 WEEKS

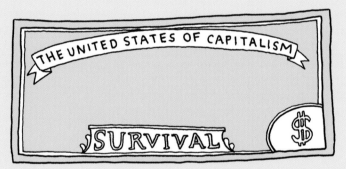
THE UNITED STATES OF CAPITALISM
SURVIVAL
$

* THIS LITTLE PIECE DOES NOT DELVE INTO THE POLITICS OF WEALTH, POVERTY, AND THEIR INEXTRICABLE INTERSECTIONS WITH RACE, CLASS, GENDER, ABILITY, AGE, AND PRIVILEGE. I COME FROM A MIDDLE-CLASS WHITE FAMILY AND THIS EXPERIENCE REFLECTS THAT.

← GENERALLY VERY ANXIOUS ABOUT MONEY

PAY TO THE ORDER OF:

THE IMPOVERISHED
THE WEALTHY
THE IMPULSIVE
THE GREEDY
THE GENEROUS
THE PERSUADED
THE COPING
THE ILL
THE BROKE
THE SAD
THE ELATED
THE HUNGRY
THE AMBITIOUS

money is complicated

AND OUR RELATIONSHIP TO IT CHANGES OVER TIME. THIS IS AN ABBREVIATED VERSION OF MINE.

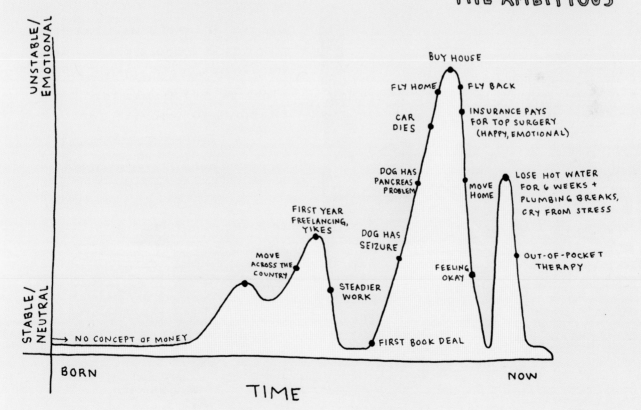

UNSTABLE/ EMOTIONAL

STABLE/ NEUTRAL

NO CONCEPT OF MONEY

MOVE ACROSS THE COUNTRY

FIRST YEAR FREELANCING, YIKES

STEADIER WORK

DOG HAS SEIZURE

FIRST BOOK DEAL

DOG HAS PANCREAS PROBLEM

CAR DIES

FLY HOME

BUY HOUSE

FLY BACK

INSURANCE PAYS FOR TOP SURGERY (HAPPY, EMOTIONAL)

MOVE HOME

FEELING OKAY

LOSE HOT WATER FOR 6 WEEKS + PLUMBING BREAKS, CRY FROM STRESS

OUT-OF-POCKET THERAPY

BORN

NOW

TIME

WEALTH IS NOT ALWAYS MONETARY AND NEITHER IS POVERTY

EMOTIONAL, SPIRITUAL, SOCIAL ~ HEALTH ~

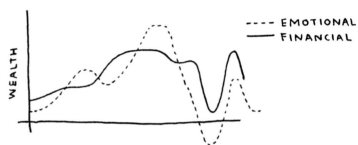

---- EMOTIONAL
—— FINANCIAL

WEALTH

SCARCITY

WORTHLESS

TOP TIER

MID-RANGE

HIGH VALUE

NEGATIVE VALUE

MEH

Twizzler

Junior Mints

Skittles

Nerds

ALL OF CHILDHOOD

WEALTHY IN TRADED HALLOWEEN CANDY THAT I WOULD KEEP IN MY SPECIAL DRAWER UNTIL IT WENT STALE BECAUSE IT WAS TOO PRECIOUS TO ACTUALLY EAT.

PAY TO THE ORDER OF ___ HALLOWEEN ECONOMICS ___ 10 SMARTIES FOR A REESE'S TRADE

AFTER MOVING 13 TIMES SINCE HIGH SCHOOL, IN JUNE 2017 I BOUGHT A HOUSE 2 MILES FROM WHERE I GREW UP. I HAD BEEN SAVING ALMOST ALL MY MONEY SINCE I WAS 16 TO BUY A HOME.

SECURITY and ACCOMPLISHMENT

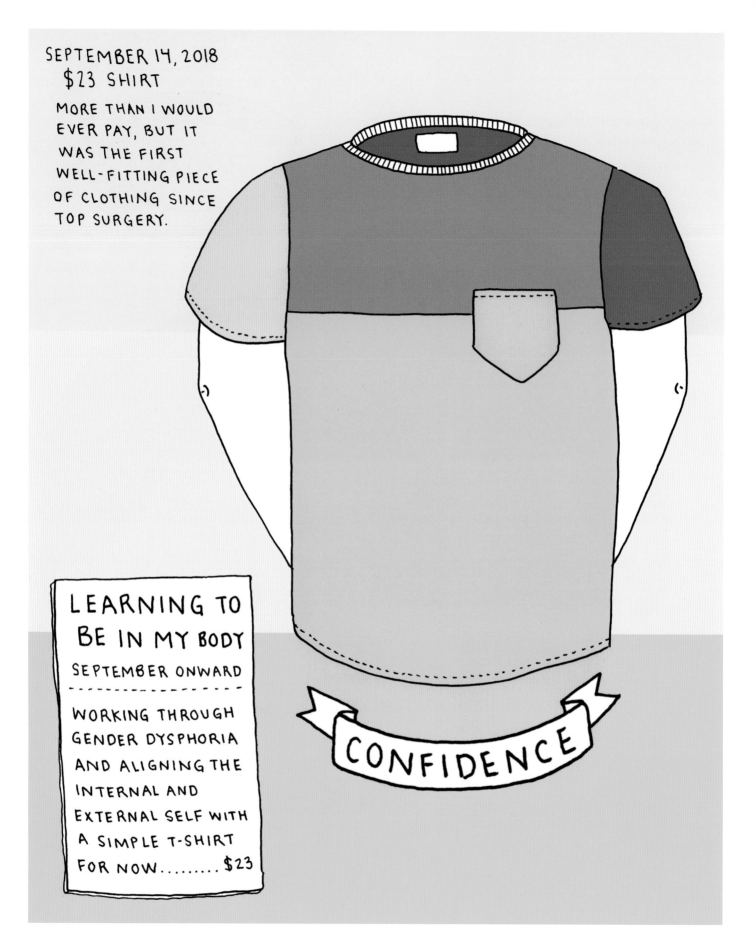

SICKNESS

2013-2014
$0.00
MY EATING DISORDER
MADE ME UNABLE TO
SPEND MONEY ON
FOOD, SO I STOLE IT.

PAY TO THE
ORDER OF __MY YOUNGER SELF__
____FORGIVENESS AND CARE____

MEMO __GROWTH__

DATE __NOW__

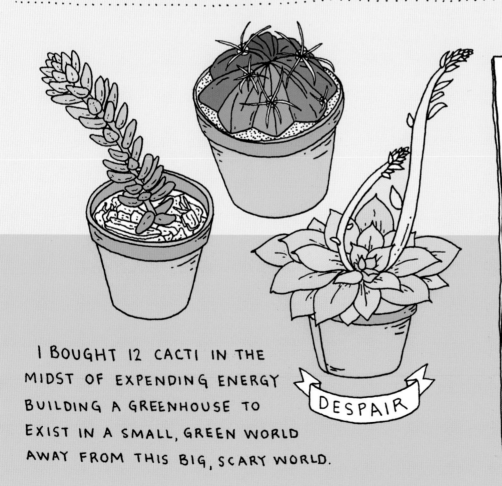

I BOUGHT 12 CACTI IN THE
MIDST OF EXPENDING ENERGY
BUILDING A GREENHOUSE TO
EXIST IN A SMALL, GREEN WORLD
AWAY FROM THIS BIG, SCARY WORLD.

DESPAIR

COPING WITH
THE SUPREME
COURT CONFIR-
MATION HEARING

OCTOBER 5, 2018
3:10 PM

WORKING THROUGH
TRAUMA $3.99

DELETING SOCIAL
MEDIA $4.99

POURING EMOTIONAL
ENERGY INTO CARING
FOR THESE PLANTS AS A
MEANS TO CARE FOR
MYSELF $11.99

FINDING JOY IN THE
NON-HUMAN $1.99

TOTAL $22.96

What Does It Take to Start a New Business?

Take a page from the unique playbooks of these four successful founders: Tania Larsson, Renee Erickson, Laila Alawa, and Eileen Rinaldi.

By Anna Watt
Illustration by Louisa Bertman

How much money do you need to get started? How long will it take before you start making a profit? Like a lot of aspiring entrepreneurs, it's questions like these that can keep you from quitting your day job in order to pursue your dream and become your own boss.

After speaking with four successful entrepreneurs and business owners—Tania Larsson, jewelry maker and indigenous artist; Renee Erickson, chef, author, and owner of Sea Creatures; Laila Alawa, CEO and founder of The Tempest; and Eileen Rinaldi, CEO and founder of Ritual Coffee Roasters—we learned it's not about the money after all. Whether you're in the first year of business or opening your seventh location, it's about having the passion and ingenuity to find out what works best for you and your business.

How did you start bankrolling your first business, for example, bootstrapped, venture capital/angel funding, business loan, crowdfunding (Kickstarter/ Indiegogo), credit cards, savings, et cetera?

Tania Larsson: I started my first business right after graduation from college with a bachelor of fine arts from the Institute of American Indian Arts. I was used to living on a tight budget, so I continued and was very strict with my spending. I moved back home with my dad, who is one of my biggest supporters. He helped me drive the 2,500 miles back from college to Northern Canada with all the second-hand equipment I needed to start my own jewelry studio in his house. I had huge community support to start my business, from my indigenous mentors gifting or trading me some equipment they were upgrading, from birthday presents made of soldering stations and rolling mills, and also from indigenous harvesters who gifted or traded me horns, antlers, or skins I could make into jewelry. I worked with my partner, who is a filmmaker and photographer, to create content for my website and social media. Collaborating with her on projects was really fun and allowed us to work together.

(Clockwise from top) Laila Alawa, Tania Larsson, Renee Erickson & Eileen Rinaldi

Renee Erickson: I was super young and borrowed 10K from my parents to buy my first business. I paid the rest as I went with a loan through the previous owner. I was terrified, so I paid it all as soon as I could. Including paying my parents back. Bootstrapped, for sure.

Laila Alawa: With every business I've launched, I have begun by putting whatever little funds I might have had at the time into the company. For example, prior to The Tempest, I ran a high-end jewelry company (Lilla Stjarna) and bootstrapped growth until we went international. When I started The Tempest, I kept operations bootstrapped and worked several jobs to ensure that I could put in the necessary funds to ensure healthy growth in the business. We successfully raised funds through a crowdfunding campaign during the beta version of The Tempest, which I carefully stretched for the next few years.

Eileen Rinaldi: The start-up capital for Ritual came from people dear to me who believed in my vision, my work ethic, and my knowledge of the industry.

Can you explain your process for building your business plan and determining a successful business model?

Tania Larsson: I had a really hard time grasping the concept of business planning. I still don't have that rigid paper that is formatted to look like a typical business plan. It really stressed me out, so I asked my sister to facilitate a visioning session with me with big flip charts, colored Sharpies, and questions I had to answer. It was imperative to understand what a successful

business meant to me, a Gwich'in woman. My long-term vision is creating opulent adornment that is connected to my culture and the land that brings us pride and makes us walk an inch taller. I also want to create content with mix-heritage indigenous people so that we can see ourselves out there, and to keep learning and revitalize my cultural practices, like tanning hides or learning old quillwork techniques.

Renee Erickson: I don't think I really had a process. Just a lot of hard work, paying close attention to the details, not skimping, being generous, and thankfully loving the business.

Laila Alawa: Oh, wow—my process for building our business plan has definitely shifted over the years, and recently I had to look at my first business plan—that was embarrassing to look at, to say the least! As a self-taught entrepreneur with an unconventional background, much of my process has been informed by advisors and online resources, which also includes getting honest, critical feedback from advisors. I firmly believe in the concept of a "living" business plan, and regularly update or iterate the plan as we move through each quarter—and that ties right into our business model: Rather than staying stale and playing it safe, I'm proud of having the honor of working with my cofounder, Mashal Waqar, and team in regularly testing and updating our business model. Just as our world—online and off—continues to change, so does our business model shift in order to reflect that. Otherwise, we'd just be setting ourselves up for failure. (And failing in order to succeed is okay—but failing due to a refusal to change? Uncool.)

Eileen Rinaldi: Well, my business is very old-fashioned in comparison to the current climate in San Francisco. I wrote a business plan based on how much it would cost to build out a café, and did projections based on how many cups of coffee I thought I could sell and wrote about who my customers would be, the market competition, threats, et cetera. I achieved my five-year plan ahead of time!

One of the biggest fears for taking the leap to start a new business is the fear of risking your quality of life, losing your financial stability, and maybe even not having access to employer benefits, such as health insurance and a 401(k). Are you able to still pay the bills, afford essentials such as health insurance, save for your retirement, and live life to the fullest? What sacrifices have you made for your business because of money?

Tania Larsson: My biggest fear in life is to not be able to practice my culture because I didn't invest time to learn from our elders and cultural carriers. This is my first year in business and I spent six weeks tanning hides as part of my work, learning from elders and working with them. I taught people at hide camps and through my social media. I traveled with my partner to ceremonies where we scheduled time for my business before and after. I created content featuring strong indigenous womxn, men, non-binary, queer, trans, and straight people. I practiced my culture by creating jewelry using materials and techniques that have been used for so long by our community. My life is so much fuller because my business allows me to

"Just as our world—online and off—continues to change, so does our business model shift in order to reflect that." —Laila Alawa

be living the dream. Financially speaking, I have healthcare because I live in the Northwest Territories, Canada. I do have a savings account. I live simply.

Renee Erickson: I think all of this is relative. We live in a world that prioritizes weather over pretty much everything else. I feel lucky to have, as well as offer, 401(k) to our employees. I am able to save. Yes, I get to live a very full life. I do work more than most I bet, but again, I really love what I do. I, too, hope to retire one day, so I am saving, but I will probably open a small retirement spot to keep busy, cooking and making places for people to gather. Can't help myself.

Laila Alawa: When I first started The Tempest, I put my nights, weekends, lunches—any possible free time—into building the company. Frankly, the fear of risking my quality of life was never something that I dwelled upon as I began spending more time—eventually leaving my day job and using what little I'd saved up to survive—on the company. Quite simply, my life is very much mission driven, and sacrificing employer benefits or office "perks" paled in comparison to finding fulfillment in the work I do at The Tempest. That has fueled my work ethic, enabled me to raise funds, and, thanks to some very careful budgeting, I've been able to pay the bills and afford essentials.

Eileen Rinaldi: I was twenty-seven when I made the leap. I was enthusiastic to give up the stability of a job with benefits to do something I believed in. My lifestyle was really modest, and I didn't have a family to worry about providing for. I was confident

that it would all work out financially. The great thing that I learned about working ninety hours a week is that you have no time to spend any money!

Money can be stressful, and you're taking huge risks to run a business. What advice do you have for managing the financial side of your business and not letting money hold you back?

Tania Larsson: Have a clear vision of what you want to accomplish and write it down so when everything seems to fall apart you have that to keep you going. Find programs to get your business started with a strong foundation. What's really important is to understand what kind of learner you are. Learning from a business advisor about cash-flow projection while they are making me do an exercise on my own projections so they can give me their input is way better for me than reading a book. I also learn a lot from podcasts and interviews featuring female entrepreneurs. This format is perfect for when I'm in the studio working. Also, find local businesses like accountants and lawyers and call them up to see if they have any pro bono services available to help you get set up. Never be afraid to ask for things you need, and remember there are many people who want to see you succeed!

Renee Erickson: Be frugal and smart with your money. Be generous to your team. Be detail-oriented. Ask for help when you need it. It will be stressful. But not always.

Laila Alawa: It's important to regularly take a step back from the flurry of work, sit down, and assess your state of mind.

Are you running your business from a purpose-driven mind-set, or is it simply to make some quick cash? The reality is that running a start-up is a marathon, not a sprint, and I've unfortunately witnessed many companies fold as a result of mixed or unclear intentions. At the same time, however, it's important to closely track your health and state of mind. Finances are a very real part of our lives. If they begin to take a toll, it's critical to negotiate a timeline with yourself around your health and business—because ultimately, you and your health come first, point-blank, period.

Eileen Rinaldi: I think that people are either entrepreneurs or they're not. I was born an entrepreneur and I knew my business well enough that I didn't feel like I was taking too big of a risk. The best advice I ever got was that managing a business is *not* about making money, it's about managing debt. It took me a few years to really understand that. But now I live by it. Debt in personal life is risky and scary. But without debt in business, you can't do anything. My other piece of advice (something I learned the hard way) is that you have to secure money *before* you need it. If you wait until you really need the money, it's too late. **gc**

A Day in the Life
of an Artist

Behind the scenes with Philadelphia artist Ronni Nicole.

Words by Ronni Nicole
Photography by Amy Franz

Making sure these minis are Instagram ready!! Instagram is a huge part of my business and success. Most of my community found me there. Keeping them updated on what I'm doing next is made easy since all I have to do is click and post.

I used to only carve my signature on the back of each piece until my friend Amanda at Paper Afternoon made me my forever stamp. It's perfectly imperfect.

One day I may get some "real business cards" but for now, I like that they are scraps of paper from previous stationery. Nothing goes to waste when you are a small business.

*I hand-cut and -write all of my thank-you notes. I like to keep things
personal with those that support me. Nothing I make is "perfect,"
but you can tell it came from me.*

I love making my mini Ron Nicoles. They are the perfect way to say thank you. When I heard that a few folks in my community were impacted by the California wildfire I wanted to do my part to help. With the support of my community, we raised $1,100 for three families.

The artist life is not that glamorous. I work from home, so that means that most of my home is used for my day-to-day business. This is me packaging my art on my living room floor.

For those who wanted to support but were unable to afford my art, thanking them was just as important. These little minis were my way of saying thank you for showing up and helping a great cause.

This desk explains my whole way of thinking in a nutshell. On the outside, I'm a minimalist, but truthfully I'm a hoarder. My desk is always clear and cute but look at that desktop. There are at least 3,000 files cluttered together in no meaningful way. But best believe I know exactly where every file is.

The best part about having a local community is that you get to personally hang out with your fans. I make any excuse I can to visit Bridget. She has the cutest children and she is so much fun to chill with. She has been collecting my art for some time now, so I'm always happy to make a personal visit to catch up on life and see what she is up to.

Showing Bridget her new Ron Nicole piece I did in a special color to match her other one. She has a collection of my art throughout her home.

The best part of the making process is the thanking part. Being an artist is a community effort. Without a supportive community, you can't be successful. Finding ways to thank them any time you can is very important.

My husband, David, is the best assistant I can ask for, but when he asked to carry my precious unpackaged artwork, I had to remind him that no one other than me and the client touches the final piece. We both laughed. gc

CREATIVE, INC. MATEO ILASCO & CHO CHRONICLE BOOKS

Accounting for the Numberphobic FOTOPULOS

THE 9 STEPS TO FINANCIAL FREEDOM Suze Orman CROWN

THE MONEY MANUAL By Tonya Rapley

PRIYA PARKER AVERHEAD BOOKS THE ART OF GATHERING

 ART INC. Lisa Congdon CHRONICLE BOOKS

authentic success Robert Holden, Ph.D. HAY HOUSE

Bring Your HUMAN to Work Erica Keswin McGraw Hill Books

DAVE RAMSEY  THE TOTAL MONEY MAKEOVER

THE POWER OF A Positive No WILLIAM URY BANTAM

Books to Get Your Business (and Finance) Life in Order

We asked seven entrepreneurs what books they turn to when they need inspiration, motivation, and some practical advice about money and work. From guides dedicated to helping creative freelancers to step-by-step manuals for gaining financial independence, this list includes our go-to favorites to keep you company at any stage of your business.

By Grace Bonney
Illustrations by Jane Mount

1. Art, Inc: The Essential Guide for Building Your Career as an Artist **by Lisa Congdon and Meg Mateo Ilasco, ed.**

2. Creative, Inc.: The Ultimate Guide to Running a Successful Freelance Business **by Joy Deangdeelert Cho and Meg Mateo Ilasco**

These two books are part of a series that all of us at *Good Company* swear by as our must-have reads for any creative entrepreneur's library. Both editions provide that magic combination of emotional inspiration and practical, easy-to-follow advice for building a creative business or art practice. Unlike most business books, both of these editions from the Inc. series are written by working artists who understand the ups and downs of creative life, online and off. Their "we've been there and know you'll get through it, too" tone is a welcome comfort when you're working through tough business decisions.

3. Authentic Success: Essential Lessons and Practices from the World's Leading Coaching Program on Success Intelligence **by Robert Holden, PhD**

"In a time of my life and career where I am evaluating what's next, this book has made me think deeper about what success really means to me. It offers up a ton of examples of very busy people and analyzes what drives them, and makes you think about what drives you." —Joy Cho of Oh Joy! (ohjoy.com)

4. The Total Money Makeover: A Proven Plan for Financial Fitness **by Dave Ramsey**

"This book was recommended to me by my bookkeeper when she saw how much I was spending on credit card charges. Reading it shifted my paradigm about money entirely, and it both helped me set up a plan to deal with my credit card debt and helped me to think about money in a more holistic, big-picture way. I was able to glean a lot of helpful tips that I've implemented and continue to implement to help me to save money." —Justina Blakeney (justinablakeney.com)

5. The Power of a Positive No: Save the Deal Save the Relationship—and Still Say No **by Willliam Ury**

"This book completely changed the way I communicate in business, but it's also had a real impact on my personal life. Women tend to be socialized to say yes to most things, often to their own detriment— something I've definitely wrestled with. The basic principles of the book help to reframe 'no' so it's not about delivering a letdown or a blow to the other person." —Claire Mazur of Of a Kind (ofakind.com)

6. The 9 Steps to Financial Freedom: Practical and Spiritual Steps So You Can Stop Worrying **by Suze Orman**

"This is my favorite book. It taught me the importance of eliminating bad debt, having eight months of living expenses saved, and having boundaries around loaning money to friends and family. Over the years I've had my share of financial challenges, but even during those tough moments I still looked to Suze for advice on how to get back on track. Today, I'm happy to say I'm back." —Malene Barnette of Malene B Designs (maleneb.com)

7. Accounting for the Numberphobic: A Survival Guide for Small Business Owners **by Dawn Fotopulos**

"This book is a great primer for someone starting a business and trying to learn how to manage profit and loss or understand fixed versus variable costs, et cetera. In addition to this book, I also recommend reading real stories about businesses that you genuinely admire. Money decisions must be made in the context of what your business stands for, what growth you hope to achieve, and your business mission, so I find case studies to be the most engaging way to learn." —Hopie and Lily Stockman of Blockshop Textiles (blockshoptextiles.com)

8. Bring Your Human to Work: 10 Surefire Ways to Design a Workplace That Is Good for People, Great for Business, and Just Might Change the World **by Erica Keswin**

9. The Art of Gathering: How We Meet and Why It Matters **by Priya Parker**

Tina Roth Eisenberg of Tattly (tattly.com) listed Parker and Keswin's books as two of her go-to reads for business inspiration. We love the way Priya Parker argues for more face-to-face time and less time spent in boring, uninspiring meetings. Parker shares practical ideas for getting more out of your business meetings and how to inspire the people you work with to give their best. Keswin's book is a must if you are overseeing a team of any size. Her tips for keeping your team (and work space) productive and happy apply to any business type and will go a long way toward improving your business's long-term success.

10. The Money Manual: A Practical Money Guide to Help You Succeed on Your Financial Journey **by Tonya B. Rapley**

Financial independence is always at the top of our minds and Tonya Rapley's step-by-step guide to making sound financial decisions is a great way to get started organizing your personal or professional finances. With business debt (and college loans) being so common with creative entrepreneurs, we love that Rapley focuses on clever (and realistic) ways to cut down your debt and get back in control of your money. **gc**

The Real Cost of Healthcare

Insurance premiums and copays are just the beginning.

By Raven Faux

Parker Gard
Photography by Andre Larrow

Ariel Lawrence
Photography by Andre Larrow

"No one has ever sat me down to explain [health insurance]. It's so unbelievably overwhelming to dive in and try to understand it all. It's pretty terrifying to know that I honestly don't even know what I'm paying for. But it's the damn truth." —Cheyenne Gil

With lots of confusing jargon, lack of meaningful conversation, and unpredictable health conditions, it's easy to misunderstand, miscalculate, and underestimate your health expenses.

We asked four people—Cheyenne Gil, a boudoir photographer with Ménière's disease; Sonalee Rashatwar, a social worker and community organizer in good general health; Ariel Lawrence, a blogger and health advocate with type 1 diabetes; and Parker Gard, a freelance creator and producer who's a transgender man with chronic asthma—about their health histories, their finances, and how they make it work. They opened up about expenses that go beyond money, such as the emotional expense of trying to find a provider who takes you seriously or taking time off from work (if you can) to recuperate. Their answers offer insight into how our healthcare system works, or doesn't, for an array of bodies and occupations.

Personal Health- and Self-care Journeys

Taking the reins of your healthcare comes with a range of emotions and concerns. For some, it's empowering; for others, it's anxiety inducing. As we age, we learn how to listen to our bodies and discern between what feels normal for ourselves and what doesn't. Our interviewees were open and kind enough to share their experiences of becoming aware and proactive about their health- and self-care.

Cheyenne Gil: My healthcare journey started in November 2017 when I started experiencing extreme cases of vertigo that would last for up to nine hours and completely put me out of commission for days. I had fullness in my left ear, trouble hearing out of that ear, constant dizziness, and problems with balance, and every four to five days I'd have a debilitating episode of vertigo—unable to speak or open my eyes, constant vomiting, unable to move an inch without getting sick. I was overwhelmed, exhausted, feeling terrible, and unable to do my work (which is a nightmare when you own your own business and you can't just hand it off to someone else). After going to my doctor, who dismissed my experience as allergies, I was angry. I was able to get an appointment with an ENT [ear, nose, throat physician] who diagnosed me with Ménière's disease but who also didn't listen to me, remember me from one week to the next, or help me in any way other than prescribing me anti-dizziness medication. Finally, I was able to make an appointment with a specialist at UPenn, where I had an incredible experience! He helped me understand what I was going through, and also diagnosed me with vestibular migraines in addition to the Ménière's disease. Now I am able to keep my disease under control by keeping my stress levels down (daily meditation and stretching, as well as therapy), and eating a low-sodium diet when I start feeling dizzy and off-balance. For years I put off going to a doctor for any reason because of the way my GP [general practitioner] had treated me—dismissing my concerns, my pain, and sending me on my way. Now that I have to be on my own insurance, I don't have as many options for GP doctors, so it's overwhelming and difficult to find someone I'm comfortable with. (I'm still on the hunt.)

Sonalee Rashatwar: I'm not sure if I identify as being on a healthcare journey. I would call it a self-care journey. As a young child, I was put on nonconsensual diets by my parents in the name of healthcare. This ended in my early twenties, when I finally decided to never diet again, for the betterment of my emotional health. This shaped my understanding of what health was supposed to mean. Now I see many things as healthcare. I monitor my bowel movements. I try to get the amount of sleep my body needs to feel rested. I work on preparing homemade and delicious meals for myself so I can eat at regular intervals. I am sexually intimate with myself. I ask for hugs and other needs from my friends. All of these aspects are part of my healthcare. It took time for me to be able to prioritize my mental healthcare just as much as my physical healthcare. It is important to note that because of being in recovery from diet culture, my weight is not an important part of my healthcare . . . While I am probably classified as super-extreme, morbidly toxic, time-bomb obese, I am pretty healthy. I experience chronic pain and sometimes mobility issues with pain in my feet, but I rarely require visiting a doctor. I have chronic hormonal conditions, and for those I see a doctor once a year to renew my prescription, but that's about it. I rarely get sick.

Parker Gard: I grew up with chronic asthma, so regular doctor visits were a big part of my life always. I had no awareness of the cost of healthcare until after college when I was jobless, without healthcare for the first time, and still needing treatment for a chronic condition! That was a really hard time because the medication I took to control my asthma was not offered in generic form and cost almost $300 a month. So it got pretty sketchy. My girlfriend at the time was still in college and even "had a bad bout of bronchitis," so she could get inhalers for me. Eventually, I got really good healthcare through my job, but even then, once I decided to begin hormone therapy and pursue surgery options as a part of my transition, found myself in the weeds in terms of coverage, knowledge, and support. It took me almost a year of arguing and appeals to have my top surgery covered by United HealthCare. I was actually in the hospital bed being prepped for surgery and waiting for the final call.

Thankfully, it was covered! Flash forward to 2017 when I went full-time freelance, I now rely on Medicaid, which presents its own unique brand of "complicated."

Ariel Lawrence: I first became mindful of what it meant to be healthy and well when I was nine years old and choked on a slice of pizza. The incident prompted several visits to the ER, where doctors told me I was hyperventilating. After a month of refusing solid foods, followed by therapy, I visited an allergist who began treating me for asthma. This began my longest healthcare-provider relationship, one that still continues to this day. My healthcare journey grew more intense after being diagnosed with type 1 diabetes at fifteen. Because my father worked for the city, we had comprehensive insurance that afforded me great flexibility with doctors and supplies. My mother was quite involved in the selection of my endocrinologists, and adamant that I received the best care. Up until my early twenties, my parents handled supply orders, navigated insurance inquiries, and researched endocrinologists. It wasn't until I moved to Washington, DC, and began my first real-world job, that I assumed greater ownership of my care.

Two years ago, I was kicked off my dad's insurance. I'd also recently finished graduate school without any job prospects. I knew my insurance would end on the thirty-first of my birth month and, in preparation, researched options on the Marketplace website and met with a social worker to aid in my decision-making process. Still, I turned twenty-six without any coverage for the upcoming month. I felt anxious, and in many respects both professionally and health-wise, was overwhelmed by the litany of options and the reality that I would spend a month uninsured.

I relied on my parents for their guidance again. My mother took me to a Medicaid office, where I was sent back home and told to apply online. After gathering the appropriate documentation and weeks of back-and-forth, I finally received coverage. When I left my job six months ago, I was less intimidated by the possibility of being uninsured. I felt confident that I could navigate the Marketplace the second time around. I also made sure to stockpile supplies and medication before resigning, which held me over while I was uninsured.

Paying for Healthcare Expenses

There's more than one way to be insured or pay for medical expenses. Options range from self-pay, employer-sponsored coverage (also known as group health insurance), and being a dependent, to government-assisted coverage, and more. In 2016, more than 157 million people received group health insurance compared to 21 million enrolled in private insurance.

Life changes such as having children or getting a new job qualify as opportunities

continued on page 102

Cheyenne Gil
Photography by Amelia Giangiulio

to adjust health coverage. Cheyenne shares her life change: "I pay for my own health insurance, but having recently been married, I'll be hopping onto my husband's very crappy health insurance policy to save money." Before (and after) the Affordable Care Act, millions of people obtained coverage the same way Sonalee does—through her employer: "Right now I am working as a salaried sexual assault counselor, where my nonprofit contributes toward my insurance premium and a portion of my paycheck goes toward having insurance."

Government assistance programs like Medicaid have been helpful for Ariel and Parker, as well as for more than 66 million people (as of August 2018). They weren't always on Medicaid, though. Ariel recalls: "When unemployed, I've paid for my healthcare expenses via government assistance (Medicaid). At my last job, I had a generous health savings account and received a benefit card. My job covered my monthly insurance contribution as well. I was able to use it for copays and any health-related expenses that were not covered by insurance. It was a godsend." Parker is currently using Medicaid for his health coverage. Previously, he had employer-sponsored insurance: "My first full-time job came with benefits which I split with the company, then I moved to a different company. [They were super progressive] and people-focused, and there I paid nothing toward healthcare (nor did my partner at the time). Unfortunately,

after being laid off from said people-focused ethical company, I now rely on Medicaid. (Thanks, Obama!)"

Estimated Income That Goes Toward Health Expenses

Estimating health expenses can be nearly impossible. When choosing a plan, it's hard to recount regular visits and the occasional minor medical needs. There's also the issue of what's considered a health expense, especially for those, like Ariel, who had a benefits card. For example, it took until July of this year for legislation to allow menstrual-hygiene products to be eligible purchases with benefits cards. We dared to ask our participants for their estimates.

Cheyenne Gil: At this point, not very much—I avoid going to the doctor unless it's absolutely necessary. When going to different doctors because of my Ménière's I spent about $1,500 altogether out of pocket—which is nothing compared to what others have to deal with. [The average American paid $1,318 out of pocket before meeting their deductible in 2015.]

Sonalee Rashatwar: I don't know what percent of my income goes to health expenses, but if I were to include things like my groceries, my therapy copays, my vacation costs, the money it takes to keep my cat happy, I would add all of these things to what it takes to maintain my health. My formal healthcare costs are maybe one-twelfth of my income,

and that's mostly because my dentist does fancy stuff to keep my teeth feeling good.

Parker Gard: Currently zero dollars. Except for certain exceptions.

Ariel Lawrence: [I don't know.] I made sure to use my benefit card whenever possible. When unemployed and on Medicaid, my personal expenses were quite limited.

Challenges Regarding Coverage and Expenses

Money is just the beginning. From trying to understand unfamiliar health jargon to finding a compassionate provider, difficulty can be found (but not always) at every step of the healthcare-acquisition process. The prevailing message? Self-advocacy is essential.

"Finding providers in network who are not fatphobic and will take my medical symptoms seriously" is a struggle for Sonalee, echoed earlier by Cheyenne. With the added stress of being a business owner, Cheyenne opens up: "Just understanding all of it, really. No one has ever sat me down to explain it [health insurance]. It's so unbelievably overwhelming to dive in and try to understand it all. It's pretty terrifying to know that I honestly don't even know what I'm paying for—and that's a hard thing to admit in an interview like this! But it's the damn truth. When it comes to being a small-business owner, there is so much that we have to handle,

> *"I see many things as healthcare. I try to get the amount of sleep my body needs to feel rested. I work on preparing homemade and delicious meals for myself so I can eat at regular intervals. I ask for hugs and other needs from my friends. All of these aspects are part of my healthcare." —Sonalee Rashatwar*

and health insurance is one of the more overwhelming things for me, personally."

Government assistance, while helpful, is limiting when it comes to the quality of care Ariel and Parker have received in the past.

Parker explains, "Initially when I first had to deal with my own insurance as an adult, the biggest challenge was advocating for my gender transition to be covered. As mentioned above, I had to have letters from therapists, other doctors, and still it meant calls, letters, and appeals in order to receive the coverage I needed. Being on hormone therapy requires me to see a doctor every few months for both bloodwork and refills. But for a while I hit a really smooth path. Having benefits through work and having already had surgeries related to my gender identity, going every few months was fine. I had a great doctor who was super knowledgeable about trans healthcare; it was sweet! However, now that I rely on government assistance, the biggest challenge is having to leave trans-friendly doctors for healthcare providers that accept Medicaid, and in my experience, that means having a pool of doctors who are alarmingly unaware of trans healthcare and sometimes downright discriminatory or offensive. In short, in order to have affordable coverage,

I had to forgo comprehensive and ongoing healthcare for my transition. Not sweet!"

"I've spent the majority of my diabetes life with great coverage and access to preferred medications and supplies," Ariel begins. "The last two years, however, have been a mixed bag. While having insurance is a privilege, and I'm grateful for Medicaid, I've learned a lot about persistence, patience, and self-advocacy while being on it. In terms of my management, there are certain supplies—for example, meters, test strips, et cetera—that are compatible with the insulin-pump therapy I use. On Medicaid, however, there are preferred brands and testing restrictions that often result in my requests being denied or leave me feeling that I don't have enough supplies to ensure the best possible care. In order to receive what I need to manage my diabetes well, I've gotten quite comfortable pushing back and requesting medical overrides."

Sacrifices Made to Cover Health Costs
Just like our DNA, everyone's combined financial and health situation is unique. Sonalee is one of the 60 percent of Americans enrolled in employer-sponsored health insurance. While she enjoys the work she does that affords her coverage, not all are as fortunate.

Ariel shares, "After graduate school, I was eager to gain full-time employment so that I could have private insurance. In retrospect, the job wasn't the best fit, but at the time I was desperate to have the insurance."

On the other hand, Cheyenne pays out of pocket for her insurance and other health costs. "As a small-business owner, I'm always making huge sacrifices to make enough money just to make ends meet! Missing family events like weddings and funerals so that I can work, overbooking myself every single week when I'm actually supposed to be doing less work to keep my stress level down, and of course, budgeting," Cheyenne explains. "Only spending money on things we absolutely need and then feeling tremendous guilt when I spend money on something I want, like a trip or a nice dinner out. I've been very fortunate because the disease I have does not require me to make frequent trips to the doctor, a specialist, or the hospital, and after the initial tests I've been able to regulate it on my own at home."

Parker has also paid out of pocket: "In certain circumstances, or out of sheer frustration, I've paid out of pocket to see a doctor who specializes in trans healthcare."

Changes That Would Improve Healthcare for All

Everyone interviewed agrees on one thing: Access to healthcare needs expansion. Cheyenne, Sonalee, and Parker believe that universal healthcare is the answer to improve America's healthcare system. "It blows my mind," Cheyenne says. "And again, I have it good. I can't imagine having a more serious chronic illness, disease, disability, cancer, et cetera. It's heartbreaking and terrifying that in general we put money over people." Sonalee points to socialism and expands on universal healthcare: "Free comprehensive healthcare for all; even undocumented folks, incarcerated folks, sex workers, fat folks, trans folks, and drug users."

Parker agrees: "On the whole, I believe healthcare should just be free for all citizens. There are so many examples of other countries that offer free healthcare and did so thoughtfully and sustainably. Personally, in the wake of the latest hateful and cruel policies proposed by the Trump administration, I am personally really scared about how said policies might affect me. There is a world in which my access to hormones is denied and, apart from transition and because of my own circumstances, my body cannot produce hormones on its own. So I need access. A policy* like this passing will see immediate, devastating, and fatal results. Healthcare should be free for every person in this country. This isn't a problem we need to solve, it's a choice we need to make."

Ariel's stance advocates for more access, but from a different angle. She elaborates: "I've read several stories about people with diabetes either rationing their insulin or succumbing to diabetic keto-acidosis because they couldn't afford it. I find it troubling that the average price of insulin nearly tripled between 2002 and 2013. Though there are programs like the Affordable Insulin Project that offer tools and resources to those seeking financial support, I wish more individuals knew about them. Additionally, I wish more states would expand their Medicaid programs. I have a dear friend living with type 1 diabetes who recently aged out of her parents' insurance after finishing graduate school. Because her state does not guarantee Medicaid based on income or disability alone, she is ineligible. Thankfully, she's been able to receive coverage through her mother's insurance and the COBRA continuation program. I often wonder, though, what if COBRA was not an option for her? How would she receive the medication and supplies she needs to survive?"

A memo from the Department of Health and Human Services circulated among media outlets. It implies the Trump administration's intention to change the definition of sex in order to revoke protections for transgender people under Title IX. **gc**

WHO ♥'S COMMUNITY COLLEGE? THIS GIRL!

You might not think of going to community college to study ART, but I did, and you know what? I loved it.

LIBBY VANDERPLOEG

ART HISTORY I & II

EXPERIMENTAL WATERCOLOR

DRAWING I & II

PHOTOGRAPHY

FIGURE DRAWING

MODERN ART HISTORY

OUTDOOR PAINTING

Of course, one deciding factor was that the tuition was relatively affordable. But I was pleasantly surprised by how much studio time I got there. Even though it wasn't technically "Art School," I spent most of my class time there painting, drawing, or learning about art history.

I also really loved the diversity of the students in my classes. Many were taking art as an elective and had an interesting and different perspective on the things we studied.

Some were professional artists, some Sunday painters, some moms and dads, and some were just trying to figure out what to be when they grew up, like me.

I loved the friendships I made in those studios, a couple of which have lasted for over 20 years now.

And there were some really cool travel abroad opportunities through community college too! I had the joy of traveling to Greece with my fellow art students, painting outdoors, and studying ancient art and architecture.

The other nice thing about community college was that the campus was close to my parents' house, so I had the option to save more money by living with them, which I did my last semester (to save money for my next move...Chicago.!).

I know there are dozens of awesome art schools out there doing a great job preparing artists and creative people for their futures.

But there are also a ton of little, affordable ones out there, like Grand Rapids Community College, that are doing an amazing job too!

That's why this working artist is proud to be

COMMUNITY COLLEGE STRONG.

LVP

The Cost of Being Disabled

Disabled people often experience discrimination in the hiring process, but meeting an employer that believes in your ability to do the job is only half the battle.

By Imani Barbarin

Sitting in an office in Midtown Manhattan, I'm breathing heavily from climbing three flights of stairs. Like many buildings in the city, it's not accessible. But I planned for this; I got here an hour early, just in case this was the case. I scoped out the building as best I could, but this type of information doesn't exist.

Equal opportunity disclosures benefit employers, not applicants. I look around the room and see beautiful girls wearing heels that perfectly complement their outfits. I'm in sneakers that make me stick out. And then there're the crutches, which gleam like a neon sign in Vegas that says, "I'm Expensive."

My interviewer comes to get me and looks shocked to see me. He appears to cover this up, likely quickly making a mental note to fire the staircase that was meant to keep people like me out. He has a motivational poster on the wall of his office that says *The only disability is a bad attitude.* Clearly, it's the excellent outlook that turns the three flights of stairs to his office into a magic broom that I lacked in getting there. We make small talk, but he never asks me about my résumé. I try to work my achievements into the conversation, but all I get is a condescending "good for you." He says he'll call if he decides to take my application further. He doesn't call. Maybe I have an attitude problem.

Finding Work That Works

I've spent the better part of my life trying to come to terms with who I am as a disabled person, but nothing makes me more acutely aware of what the world thinks of a Black disabled woman quite like a job interview. Sitting in waiting areas thinking of how I can downplay or make a joke or (God help me) present myself as inspiring to the person in front of me so they take another look at my résumé is not how I anticipated spending huge chunks of my time as a kid. To their credit, my parents tried to warn me, "You will have to work twice as hard to get half as far." But, against my better judgment, and the entirety of my life experience, I find myself falling back into optimism time after time.

About two years ago, when I was weighing my decision to attend graduate school, I struggled with the prospect of just how much opportunity would be available to me upon graduation and whether or not it

Ajani AJ Murray
Photo by Lynsey Weatherspoon

was quite worth it. I jumped, and semester after semester, I saw graduates in the classes ahead of me juggle awesome job opportunities as a voice in the back of my head reminded me that the same would be a stretch for me. I faithfully got a head start on the job-application process, filling out several a full six months before my graduation to familiarize recruiters and hiring managers with my résumé. Ever the dutiful applicant, I made sure to disclose my disability in the equal opportunity section. In six months of applying for jobs with a goal of fifteen applications a week, I received only one call inquiring about my résumé. Once I stopped disclosing, however, I was able to secure six interviews within a week.

My experience is not an isolated anecdote, and according to the Bureau of Labor Statistics, the unemployment rate for disabled people is double that for the able-bodied. While the passing of the Americans with Disabilities Act gave disabled people protections against discrimination in the workplace, the law did little to change the attitudes of the general public toward them.

While getting in the door is a hassle, it's only half the battle. Sometimes getting the job means compounded financial constraints that can lead to losing health insurance for those self-employed, restricting personal opportunities like marriage, or leaving hard-won employment because of a lack of accessibility, discrimination, or income that's too high to keep assisted health coverage.

With all that is stacked against disabled people, employment can seem daunting and financial stability out of reach. But even with the acknowledged difficulties, there are disabled people managing jobs and independence.

Gregg Beratan

Gregg Beratan, who is the manager of government affairs at the Center for Disability Rights, feels fortunate to be employed. He hated the job search, feeling as though the entire process triggered imposter syndrome—as if he were taking advantage of all the executive-functioning issues he's spent a lifetime dealing with. During his last unemployed period, he spent nearly a year looking for work while working freelance—taking editing gigs to make ends meet.

Once he landed a position, it was an excellent match. "I am blessed to work in a disability-led organization that is very good about accommodating employees. I have never felt more supported and embraced by an employer."

While acknowledging the additional financial burden placed upon disabled people simply for being, he admits that most people are still reeling from the recession. "I think in the post-crash economy, everyone's finances feel tenuous and insecure. I can't say disability shapes that, particularly."

With experience living abroad, Beratan found it insightful that the government in the United Kingdom made a disabled living allowance available to people with disabilities in an effort to mitigate some of the financial stresses. "I do wish people understood the additional costs placed on disabled people, because ableism in society [means people haven't] considered us or have chosen to ignore us."

With so many things functionally out of reach for disabled people, the cost of access comes from their pockets. "Accessibility is an afterthought to so many people. There are so many additional costs."

Alice Wong
Photo by Alora King Villa LeMalu

Gregg Beratan
Photo by Tony Luong

Rebecca Cokley

When Rebecca Cokley left her position at the end of the Obama administration, she had a plan. After serving for the entirety of the administration, she took careful steps to transition and give herself an opportunity to decide what was next. Knowing exactly how much financial flexibility she had in looking for a job, Cokley took a job as the director of the Disability Justice Initiative at the Center for American Progress.

Like Beratan, Cokley felt well received by her new workplace. Many disabled people who have jobs feel as though they are either outright denied accommodations or are slowly pushed out of their positions once employers become aware of the additional costs associated with assistive technology. (It's important to note that the ADA legally requires workplaces to make accommodations available to disabled employees.) Gratefully, this time, that was not the case. "My boss has been an ally of the disability community for a long time and was very open to talking to me about what accommodations I needed, and I didn't face any pushback," says Cokley, who transitioned from consulting to this full-time position.

Like many disabled people, the health insurance associated with employment was nonnegotiable. With herself, her husband, and two of her three children disabled, high-quality insurance was a necessary part of her job decision.

For Cokley, the financial cost of being disabled comes from navigating a world designed for able or normative bodies. "[Little people] pay twice as much for a wardrobe because you're having to pay for alterations. If the airline breaks your wheelchair or loses your cushion, you will likely need to offset that cost on your own while you fight to get reimbursed, or you aren't able to go to work." What seem to be insignificant costs add up for disabled people, which can affect not only their wallets but their careers as well.

Ajani AJ Murray

Where many consider their disability a hindrance to their employment, Ajani AJ Murray gets hired because of his. As an actor, freelance consultant, and public speaker, the work has been sporadic but has given him multiple opportunities, including guest appearances on ABC's *Speechless* and Comedy Central's *Drunk History.*

While represented by a talent agent, he finds networking instrumental in his ability to land jobs, though he admits that it hasn't been enough to reach financial independence. "Being disabled is expensive! I have never worked in these past five years a consistent twelve months or consecutive years. My income affects my SSI, which I still rely on," Murray relays. For disabled people who rely on Social Security Income, having a monthly income higher than $1,180 means a loss of necessary funds ($750 per month). It gives an entirely new meaning to the phrase "living paycheck to paycheck."

Murray needs a personal aide, but financial constraints mean he doesn't have the money to cover the cost of paying an assistant. Wherever possible, he makes travel, accommodations, and accessibility a part of his contract, but he admits he is still waiting for the day when he can have more financial freedom.

"What people should know and what I had to learn myself is the hidden extra cost of living with a disability is an enormous

Rebecca Cokley
Photo by Kate Warren

stress that cripples our community and our families' lives more than the initial diagnosis," says Murray, echoing a sentiment expressed by many disability rights advocates. While a diagnosis is difficult to live with, unexpected expenses and an inaccessible society compound the issues associated with disability.

While the road for Murray has been difficult and has often felt like an "impossible dream," he has been well received. "When I finally got a wheel in the door, I was received quite well . . . I've been received with open arms and many people I work with have been very receptive and sensitive to what I bring to the table."

Alice Wong

Alice Wong used to have a "regular" job as a university-staff research associate but wanted more flexibility and left to devote themself to activism and media making. They currently work as a freelance research consultant. Alongside their numerous speaking engagements, this comprises a majority of their income, but it is far from consistent. Because of Medicaid rules, Wong is stuck in a poverty trap. "I worry constantly about the total amount I will earn annually because I must report this every year in order to remain eligible on Medicaid in my state." They frequently check their bank account with this in mind.

A majority of the people they work with know Wong is disabled, and for those who do not, they make it known. Wong works from home and uses email and videoconferencing to get things done. Preserving their wellness is a priority, so they often pass on assignments that strain their stamina. This means that gigs can be irregular and few and far between.

For them, the cost of living with a disability is more than financial. "It's sweating

about or forgoing jobs, opportunities, events, and options that most nondisabled people don't even have to worry about." Wong goes on to say that there will always be complex reasons why some disabled people cannot seek employment and society should accept that. They also hope that the American healthcare system becomes more flexible to allow disabled people to work without the risk of losing services.

In an ideal world, Wong wants people's values to not be tied to outmoded ideas on productivity that always portray disabled people and those who use safety net programs to survive as "lazy" or "unmotivated." They look forward to a more understanding and inclusive future. "I'd like to live in a society that allows us to reach our fullest potential, and accepts us as we are, employed or not."

Looking Forward

For many disabled people, finding a job can seem like an impossible feat, and once a job is found, the financial-juggling game starts. As disabled people are often reliant on social programs for healthcare and income, we must make enough to cover the surprise costs we often incur for accessibility while at the same time not make too much money so that we are booted from those programs. Additionally, it also doesn't help that healthcare is tied to employment at all. It means that rather than seeing disabled people according to their résumés, we're seen as higher healthcare costs to the company overall. Ironically, it is these very institutions designed to usher us into financial independence that trap us in poverty.

There is hope, though. With social media, pushes toward diversity in all aspects of American life, and talk of healthcare for all, disabled people are more visible and using their voices to bring life to their lived

experiences. Society overall is becoming more familiar with the ways in which disability intersects with poverty, and organizations focused on disability are protesting for more financial freedom. But disabled people cannot fight alone. If you want to become involved:

Follow the work of disabled-led rights organizations like National ADAPT and the Disability Visibility Project, and become familiar with the topics disabled people are talking about.

If you're thinking of starting your own business, become familiar with accessibility and what is required of you as an owner. Recognize that it's not nice, it's the law. If you're an employee concerned about inclusivity, consider being an ally to your disabled coworkers. Always approach the situation with the knowledge they can say no, but should they accept, it can be a huge relief for them. Listen to their needs and help wherever possible, but don't act on their behalf without their knowledge or permission.

Pay attention to your local elections and vote. Disabled people intersect with every single demographic, and we experience bias starting at childhood, so even a school board election can trickle into a disabled person's ability to get work later in life.

Nondisabled people need to be willing to listen to the community and hold elected officials accountable for protecting disability rights. In this regard, it's time for nondisabled people to get to work. **gc**

An Immigrant's Money Mind-set

How limiting beliefs keep us safe in scarcity when we are meant to thrive in abundance.

By Bruna Nessif
Photo collage by Clare Celeste

As the desire for financial freedom continues to rise for immigrants, so does the glaring reality that limiting beliefs surrounding money fed from childhood have played a role in stunting our potential. But money is the root of all evil. Right?

I grew up feeling like anything revolving around money was taboo. Talking about it felt dirty. Wanting a lot of it felt dirty.

Asking for it back felt dirty. So in an effort to not feel dirty all the time, I'd just ignore its existence, and the lack of overflowing money in my life made that very easy to practice.

As an immigrant, I grew up like many other families who migrated here in hopes for a better life. My parents scraped by, working jobs they didn't care for but would never complain about doing,

because it meant a roof over our head, food on the table, and clothes on our back. (Who cares if it was from Goodwill and not Nordstrom?) Regardless of how little we had, it was something, and when you're in a position that makes you feel like you should be grateful for whatever you're able to get, something feels like luxury.

Still, I wanted more than just something. I wanted to feel like I deserved more than

Regardless of how little we had, it was something, and when you're in a position that makes you feel like you should be grateful for whatever you're able to get, something feels like luxury.

the bare minimum but because of my culture and upbringing, that desire for abundance disguised itself as selfishness for a very long time, so I didn't even dare entertain it.

How ungrateful must I be to want more than what I've been blessed with?

When you come from a place of lack, you don't see it as lack at first. You see it as a blessing, because "it could always be worse." You begin to idolize limiting beliefs that prance around as truths, and suddenly phrases like "I have to work hard to make money" or "More money, more problems" begin to form as mantras to your life, and you convince yourself that money is not easily accessible and riddled with consequences. But once you're able to see beyond the limitations that are not only fed to you, but digested by your subconscious and therefore practiced in your daily life, you realize that your relationship with money is the main reason you're not in a place of financial freedom.

I began grappling with this concept as a young adult. I was always smart with my money—thanks to my mother's constant lessons about saving what I earned—and while I was grateful for her knowledge on staying debt-free and avoiding interest rates whenever possible (which were never discussed in the classroom, of course), I

was also aware that I was clinging to whatever I had so tightly, because I never felt as though money would make its way back to me, and that energy was actually blocking me from reaching my full potential financially.

In Jen Hemphill's book, *Her Money Matters: The Missing Truths from Traditional Money Advice*, she explains that the traditional money skills (such as budgeting, saving, making money, dealing with debt, et cetera) take up only 10 percent of our money brain space, meaning that's just one small sliver of the pie when it comes to accessing financial abundance.

So, while I was killing it in that department, it became clear that there was more work to be done, because I wasn't seeing the outcome I'd hoped. So what else did I need to do?

According to Hemphill, another 30 percent of our money brain space is dedicated to money actions. This means learning to have those uncomfortable conversations about money, the same conversations I grew up learning were disrespectful and unnecessary, so that you can begin to build your financial confidence.

Liz Hernandez, a Mexican American woman and the founder of Wordaful, a venture she decided to take on full time

after many years in the entertainment industry, tapped into her money actions when she realized it would become necessary for her well-being. That doesn't mean it was easy, though.

"My parents were great at communicating to us that we had value in the world and they emphasized that nothing comes easy, especially money. I was to work hard, be humble, and ask to be paid fairly," she explains.

"It made sense, except that wasn't my experience in corporate America, especially when negotiating a contract. My father always encouraged me to speak up, but it felt like I was stepping out of line since, as a child, I watched my grandmother and mother work extremely hard in their households without asking for much except respect from their children. As a first-generation woman in the workplace, my need to speak up was getting caught in the crosshairs of my values of being respectful and polite."

However, for Liz, that value of being respectful and polite in the workplace was getting overshadowed by one glaring reality.

"I put in years of hard work at a job where it was made painfully evident I was never going to be paid fairly. It didn't just affect my livelihood, it hurt my morale watching my male coworkers purchase homes and cars, and raise families while I was making just enough to pay rent and take care of life necessities," Hernandez states.

"I took a meeting with my employer and asked to bring in an agent to negotiate my deal. He told me that they don't really like to deal with agents because this workplace was like a family. Being polite, I backed down and negotiated myself. Huge mistake."

While that move may not have been the best for Hernandez, she still decided to take matters into her own hands by sparking conversations about money with her peers to gain some insight.

"I had to learn as I went, but I started reaching out to other women in my field to compare work and pay. We don't always want to have these conversations, but they are important and needed. If your mother never worked in corporate, she can't share her experience with you. You have to find mentors and colleagues you can trust."

She continues, "It's important to understand that the workplace is not the same as home or family. In Latino culture, we are taught a strong sense of loyalty, and we put that energy into our workplace and in those around us. We sometimes feel bad if we're not giving more than we're taking.

This needs to change. We need to ask questions, know what our counterparts are earning, and speak up. The toughest lesson I've had to learn is that it's nothing personal, it's just business. We need to remember that saying works both ways."

The same was true for George McCalman, who, as a Black and West Indian creative director, quickly realized that there was more to money than what he was taught when he decided to open his own business, and in order to learn what was needed to succeed, he needed to step outside of his comfort zone.

"I opened my own design studio (McCalman.Co) eight years ago. I had no idea what I was doing. I learned, through making mistakes, that I had to adjust how I thought about myself as a graphic designer and artist. I had a business, and I was also responsible for making smarter decisions. The business-versus-art conflict is real. We artists can be tortured about placing value on what we do. I can tell you that I struggled with it. I didn't know what I didn't know, and I was ashamed to ask questions. That was the first change I embraced. Asking what I thought were 'dumb' questions: 'How much should I charge? When can I send invoices? What software should I use? I don't know how to deal with this client and don't think I should work with them anymore.' Those

kind of questions. That's where the smartest business decisions come from."

McCalman admits that "thinking about things like financial stability, planning for the future, and creating budgets for myself is a more recent awareness. I always thought I was better at making money than saving it. But I'm learning that I'm getting better at both."

And he hit many bumps along the road due to the fact that he didn't have anyone to teach him the ropes.

"That's why I struggled. I didn't have anyone give me those lessons when I was growing up. So I made it up. I had a boyfriend several years ago who was different from me in those ways. He grew up schooled in finances and had a system of how he related to money. I remember at the time thinking, *This is how rich people stay rich. They have systems to ensure that they do.* That was a wake-up call for me. I realized I had to relearn and define what my relationship to money was. It changed my business, and my life."

And that, ladies and gentlemen, is key.

While speaking up and asking questions, saving, paying off debt, and budgeting are important, they still only add up to 40 percent of what Hemphill says it takes to really shift your view, and therefore attraction, of money in your life. So what is this whopping 60 percent that we have yet to tap into?

She calls it your "money mind-set," and it's exactly what we've been talking about in this entire article.

Your money mind-set is about your relationship to your money. It is how you frame, relate to, and approach all aspects of money in your life, which, considering what we've discussed thus far, can be largely impacted by the way your family raised you to look at money. And unfortunately, for immigrants, that relationship is hardly ever from a place of abundance, but more likely than not, a scarcity mind-set.

As a millennial, I'm living in a time that is unlike any other. We are no longer expected to carry on traditional ways of living, like the generations before us, which also means breaking away from traditional lifestyle practices. College is no longer thought of as mandatory for success. Getting a corporate job right after college graduation is no longer the dream. Accepting whatever paycheck we're given is no longer the bar that sets the standard of what we're worth.

Now the dream is freedom—working for yourself, creating what you're passionate about, and making a living doing it. And the amount of money on those paychecks is entirely decided by you. As liberating as that sounds, the idea of actually pursuing this life can be frightening, especially when you've been made to believe that such desires are fairy tales.

Nothing tested my mentality on money more than the decision to quit my safe, corporate job to pursue my own endeavors, and nothing scared me more than the possible reaction to this decision from my immigrant parents.

I could hear them now: "We went through all of this to bring you here so you can get a college degree and not have to suffer like we did, and still you decide to leave stability and do this? What even *is* this? How will you make money?"

My assumption of their response caused me to delay my decision until I just couldn't fake the funk any longer. Luckily, when the conversation actually happened, their response was supportive, even if they didn't entirely understand why I would let go of such stability (aka an immigrant's biggest goal) to dive into the unknown. So, here I was. I was tapping into the 40 percent of my money brain, but my deep-rooted unhealthy relationship with money continued to chime in and throw me off course, no matter how carefully I'd budget

or how much firmer my voice was when delivering my rate to clients.

Society has done a great job at making us feel like we shouldn't talk about money, which has created silence around a topic that is very crucial to discuss, and that is why many people don't even step outside the 10 percent Hemphill describes. Additionally, Corporate America has done a seamless job in making you feel privileged to be earning whatever it is you're making, even if you feel you deserve more. Pair that with cultural pressures and traditions about accepting what's given to you with grace and gratitude, and the guilt trip to want more for yourself can shut you up quick.

Until you realize that it's all in your head.

Money guru and founder of My Fab Finance Tonya Rapley tells me that in order to change your mind-set about money, it's crucial to "commit to understanding what limiting beliefs you have around money, create a narrative that counteracts those limiting beliefs, and then remind yourself of that narrative that you're using to counteract on a regular basis."

She continues, "Put yourself in a position where you're identifying all the ways that your limiting beliefs are wrong instead of right, because a lot of times we try to

We are not just here to achieve the American dream. We are *the American dream*.

validate our limiting beliefs with things that happen instead of finding every reason to discredit what those beliefs are."

Rapley also notes that the most common misconceptions about money for immigrants are that "money equals happiness and that stability will equal happiness, when that is not always the case. People can be miserable and financially secure at the same time. People could live happily and be financially insecure."

She also touches on the pressures that can arise from immigrant households when it comes to schooling and career. "I think there is this notion that hard work and education equal financial success, and that doesn't always balance out. I've seen a lot of my clients who are children of immigrants go to school to pursue this American dream, or go to college to pursue this American dream, to attain these career paths that are highly praised in most immigrant communities, only to graduate with large amounts of debt that they're unable to manage. Now they have this career that their parents are proud of, but they also have this debt that is stifling for them. [They] think that education equals economic freedom, which isn't always the case."

Rapley concludes, "Challenge the beliefs that you have and prove otherwise. I like to call them little magic tricks. Sometimes

I'll say, 'I want to experience this, or I want to accomplish this, or I want my money to do this for me.' Just seeing that happen and continuously doing these little tricks and continuously seeing them happen reaffirmed my faith and belief in abundance and helps to reduce some of those limiting beliefs that I've had. But everybody has them, and everybody has to work to counter them regularly."

As children of immigrants, or even immigrants ourselves, we are raised with a certain mind-set when it comes to money that, for all intents and purposes, is centered around stability and security, and that makes complete sense given the situation. However, when we begin to notice that this "safety" we've strived for is actually stunting our potential for financial abundance, it's time to change the narrative.

This is both extremely simple and difficult at the same time. Some might hear, "Oh, so I just have to change my thoughts about money? Easy," and you'd be right. But the challenge there is not just shifting your mind-set and maintaining it but first becoming aware of the ideas you hold so close about money that you may not even notice. What are you saying to yourself on a daily basis when it comes to finances? How do you feel whenever money is brought up in conversation? What are

your first thoughts when it's time to pay the bills?

It is very taxing to not only stray away from the beliefs you were taught from a young age but branch out into uncharted territory on a subject that is so important without much guidance or clarity. But if you were told that these limiting beliefs are the big blocks stopping you from achieving financial success your family has yet to experience, don't you think it's worth seeing what would happen without them?

The love and pride that run through our veins for our family and culture are thick and noble, but it is our duty to evolve as individuals and as a generation so that we may continue to pave a way for those who come after us. And sometimes, in order to do that, we need to break away from the cycle of fruitless practices based in scarcity and fear that were passed down with the best of intentions but that no longer serve us, because we are not just here to achieve the American dream. We *are* the American dream. **gc**

From coast to coast, nine drag queens and kings tell us what it's really like to make a living as a drag performer.

By Grace Bonney
Illustration by Lauren Tamaki

Around the world, drag performers are some of the most exciting and exhilarating performers you'll find on any stage. These multitalented, multi-hyphenate artists have mastered the arts of performance, surprise, innovation, and creativity.

A typical drag show involves elements of fashion and beauty, like hand-rhinestoned tights, triple-stacked custom eyelashes, and elaborately contoured five o'clock shadows, as well as performance: carefully choreographed dance and burlesque routines. Queens and kings are also some of the most creative collaborators in our community, often working with teams of creative artists (makeup, wigs, nails, and fashion) or drag families that help them create looks and routines to stand out.

While drag has become more popular with mainstream audiences thanks to television shows like *RuPaul's Drag Race*, not all drag performers are treated—or paid—equally. Issues of gender, race, and class cut through the drag world like any other community and affect every aspect of a performer's career. We sat down with nine performers from across the United States to talk about the true cost of drag, the best (and worst) parts of performing, and how fans can support their favorite kings and queens in ways that actually make it easier for them to make a living doing what they love.

The Cost of Drag

The money that queens and kings put into their looks can vary wildly from performer to performer. But one sentiment rings true across the board: Most drag fans don't realize just how many hidden costs exist in drag. Legendary drag performer **Miss Coco Peru** summarized it well when she told us, "I think Dolly Parton said it best when she said, 'You'd be surprised how much it costs to look this cheap.'"

Hair and Makeup

Sara Andrews, a queen from Chicago (and the founder of Wig Takeout), explained the quickly escalating costs of drag performances, "Back in the day, I could make a costume with $1-per-yard fabric from Walmart for $10. Now I spend about $300-plus for a designer to make something nice for me. Even if I do make something for myself, good fabric alone can cost at least $100-plus. Luckily, I can do my own wigs, so I don't have to spend another $300 on that. But a good base wig can still cost $100 or so. Of course there are cheaper options. But you get what you pay for."

Creme Fatale of Los Angeles says that her outfits typically cost several hundred dollars. "My outfit will cost a few hundred at least, $200 to $300. Wigs are two-stacked wigs, minimum, plus the cost of styling. Another $200. Shoes are $50. I also buy props, around $100. But I am a drag queen, and things must be rhinestoned! Quality rhinestones for my outfit and shoes average $50 to $60. [Altogether that is] about $600 to $700."

Queens and kings who have had the opportunity to perform on television often have access to higher budgets for performance outfits—and are expected to look like they do, as well. Brooklyn's **Aja**, who starred in two seasons of *RuPaul's Drag Race*, often spends thousands of dollars on a single dress. "[Performance cost] depends on the style of the person, it depends on the resources, and it also depends on the budget of the person. I have spent $6,000 on a dress and $4,000 on a burlesque routine, but then have spent $10 on a stretch dress from up the block. It really depends on what the person is going for. But 'good drag' (which is an artificial standard, thanks to the *RuPaul's Drag Race* fandom) is expensive, nonetheless. Queens are often compared and told they look bad or cheap, and unfortunately sometimes they're not eating [so they can afford to] give a look."

For drag kings, like **Pretty Rik E** (coproducer of Pretty Boi Drag in Washington, DC), costs are significant as well and aren't helped by the fact that drag kings don't typically receive equal pay or attention from the drag industry and audiences. "I was completely broke when I decided to give drag a try and was forced to actually pawn some personal items so I could purchase an outfit for the show. I can spend as much as $200 on an outfit alone. I may spend more if the act is intended to be a signature act (an act that I will perform over and over again). But this doesn't include makeup, which can run anywhere from $20 to $60, depending on how much I'm planning to wear."

No matter what a performer makes during the course of the show, oftentimes they can expect to spend as much, if not more, on their production. **Soju**, a queen from Chicago, said, "Basically whatever you make from a gig or a show, you're using five times more on your drag. Custom hair, dresses, makeup, and travel [add up]. The list goes on, but we make it work somehow. I will say, though, these are all investments and you can reuse and make it worth your while if you take care of your drag and do a lot of shows."

Performances
The cost of drag isn't only about hair, makeup, and outfits—it also includes the cost of the scenery and setup around any given performance. San Francisco queen **Peaches Christ** explained, "My shows aren't necessarily the average drag performance. We're building sets, creating video, doing lighting designs, renting equipment, and performing special effects, so the budget gets extremely robust."

Hidden Costs
While the cost of forward-facing elements of a drag performance may be more obvious to fans, there are many elements of drag that are equally burdensome but not often understood by the audience.

Coco Peru explained, "I think people who don't know drag queens personally don't see how much time and effort goes into creating your persona and show. When I have had people watch the process of me getting into drag (and they see the suitcases filled with everything it takes and the time it takes), they have a new respect for that aspect of it. Although an audience sees an hour-and-fifteen-minute show, they don't see the traveling, they don't see the sound checks, the showering and shaving, the setting up your makeup and costumes,

> # "*Doing drag comes with costs that some people don't realize. Not everything is material or money related. Sometimes [the costs] are your friends and family, your self-esteem, and your patience.*" —Aja

the hour or two getting into drag, and the time it takes to pack all that back up, get back to your hotel, and then begin the process of removing all of the stuff. So, not even including the time traveling around the country, it can turn into an eight- or nine-hour workday for that hour-and-fifteen-minute show, and as they say, 'Time is money.'"

Bob the Drag Queen, winner of season eight of *RuPaul's Drag Race*, summed up the biggest expense most performers noted: car services. "Transportation is actually a lot more expensive than people think it is. Ubers are a lot of money."

Heklina, a legendary queen from San Francisco, added, "A drag queen can't just hop on a bus or take a bicycle to the gig!"

Soju discussed another huge cost for performers traveling with costumes and supplies: "Baggage fees can run up in *hundreds* if you don't pack lightly, and let's be honest: WE ARE DRAG QUEENS."

Not all hidden costs are financial, though. **Aja** added, "Doing drag comes with costs that some people don't realize. Not everything is material or money related. Sometimes [the costs] are your friends and family, your self-esteem, and your

"You just have to get your face and name out there if you want to make this your full-time job. Be ready to work hard in and out of drag." —Soju

patience. People will praise someone who has spent one-tenth of what they have but look amazing on the surface. People will also bash and chastise a queen who has given everything they have because that person is not seen as enough."

Making a Living
Like most artists in the creative community, drag performers have all had to diversify their revenue streams to make a living in their chosen field.

Soju explained, "It's hard to make a full-time living in drag unless you're down to hustle until you have basically no life except for drag. Unless you're a Ru Girl, you will have to do multiple shows a week, maybe even a day, to just get by. I started making YouTube videos, which helped bring in attention to my drag, which then helped me get booked with a higher booking fee. You just have to get your face and name out there if you want to make this your full-time job. Be ready to work hard in *and* out of drag."

Peaches Christ echoed what so many performers noted, that being in control of your own image and content is key. "For me, it became clear that I had to produce my own events, write my own content, make my own movies, and build my own audience in order to make a living. By being my own producer, I control the budget and am able to create my own revenue stream."

Heklina agreed with Peaches: "I am a producer, and when it comes to drag you *have* to be a producer or promoter if you expect to make money at all."

Performances
While live performances aren't the only way most performers stay afloat, they are still the bread and butter of many queens and kings. But their pricing and structure can swing wildly, depending on a number of factors. **Creme Fatale** explained, "Your fee can vary from club to club and varies greatly based on your social media popularity and presence. When performing, you make tips. Tips vary depending on the club, the day of the week, and on how you are performing."

Pretty Rik E noted that production has a lot to do with how performers make a living, too. "As a producer, my job is to create the space for other kings to not only put on great performances but also to pay them a reasonable fee for performing. It is also my job to make it easy for an audience to tip performers, so we will bring hundreds of dollars in cash for tipping to take the burden off of the venue and the audience to bring their own. If done right, a performer *should* walk out with more money in tips than their base pay."

Some queens, like **Coco Peru**, focus on booking their shows where there is no rental fee so they can have more control over the profits. While some performers arrange a profit split with the venue, some ask to be paid a flat salary. And no matter where performances take place, most performers make at least some portion of their income on merchandise and paid interactions with fans, like meet and greets or cameos (where fans can pay a fee to receive customized video messages).

Creme Fatale has diversified her income stream even further. "In addition to performing, I have a Patreon page where I upload tutorials for fans that pay monthly for content. Various companies also send me products [to use online] and give me discount codes, which provide me with a cut of sales."

Branching Out

While some performers are known for lip-synching, some drag artists produce and record their own content (music, comedy, et cetera) that they can also have as part of their own personal drag economy.

"My art falls more into the music realm now, so I make money off of my music sales, streams, and shows," explains **Aja**. "However, when I was doing more drag-based performances, it was easy to support myself. Even without television, I was doing okay. It wasn't the best, but it was comfortable. I think how much money an artist makes really depends on what kind of performance they are doing. My biggest advice is to find the right venues for your type of performance."

Discrimination and Pay Equity

Like most artistic fields, the world of drag is affected by biases, prejudice, and systemic problems. "Drag is a microcosm of the outside world, so a lot of the things that happen in the outside world happen also in drag," explained **Bob the Drag Queen**. "[That includes] women being paid less to do drag than men are; that includes trans women as well."

Gender

The majority of performers I spoke with noted that cisgender and transgender women are often paid less and have less audience and media support.

Sara Andrews shared her personal story as a transgender woman and drag performer: "Trans queens were once very highly revered in this industry. It has been one of the few industries in which we could succeed. When I started transitioning in the Bible Belt in the early 2000s, no one would hire me. Historically speaking, there have been two professions in which trans women could openly flourish: One is sex work, and the other is drag. Luckily for me, I was an amateur drag queen long before I started transitioning. So I was able to break into it professionally once finding a day job became impossible. Other girls aren't always so lucky. *RuPaul's Drag Race* has created a caste system and a glass ceiling that trans women cannot break. I've known quite a few [trans women] who put off transitioning in hopes of getting their big break [on the show] first. I've all but given up on what now seems like a dead-end career for a transsexual queen like myself. So I now own a successful wig-styling business (Wig Takeout) for drag queens and support myself and my fifteen-year profession (now turned hobby) by selling pieces of my art to other queens."

Creme Fatale added, "I am a cisgender Latina woman who doesn't possess a thin body frame. Many successful drag queens are thin, white, cisgender men. Trans women have always played a huge role in the drag community but have not seen much representation in the mainstream drag community. Many talented trans and cisgender men and women struggle to find success in the current age of drag, where the most praised and booked queens are drag queens that have been featured on television." **Heklina** echoed this sentiment and added, "Most cities are not as forward thinking and have not embraced the concept of [cisgender] queens."

For drag kings, gender discrimination is a huge part of the challenge they face in making a living as performers. **Pretty Rik E** noted that "because drag kings aren't as socially recognizable as drag queens, you have to be willing to fight for the space to perform, as well as a decent fee. It is even more difficult for drag kings of color. There are far fewer of us, and sometimes the space is not set up to be a safe space for us (like white performers performing inappropriate or appropriative acts). A recent example is a local university asked us to put together a few drag kings for a show they were doing. When we asked about pay, they told us the only people getting paid were their headliners, who were all queens. This happens far too often and greatly affects how we, as kings, are able to be paid for our work."

Race

Race is another huge factor when it comes to performers and the opportunities (and pay scales) they see in the drag economy. "It is without a doubt way harder for artists of color in the drag world to become successful," said **Aja**. "I remember when I first came out into the scene, there were a lot of white queens who would not work with me. I was accused of stealing and causing a commotion at times when I wasn't up to anything out of the ordinary. I feel like this forces people of color to have to assimilate to a behavior that non-POC people deem to be acceptable. If someone cannot do this, then unfortunately, it becomes difficult for them to find work."

Soju agreed, adding, "I notice that lighter-skin queens get by with a lot less. I can't help but notice that if you're skinny and white, you can pretty much wear whatever you want and people will most likely tip you and praise you. Bigger girls and queens of color have fewer opportunities to shine and work in this industry. That's why we have to work extra hard and be literally *extra* to be booked. That's the tea on that."

Creme Fatale noted, "The truth is that white drag queens tend to receive the most adoration from fans, while queens of color tend to receive racial backlash for anything they do. Backlash and criticism affect bookings greatly, directly affecting finances. These are all conversations that are actively being had in the drag community, so there is hope that things will change."

How to Support Queens and Kings
If you're inspired by the excitement, beauty, and artistic expression of drag performers, there are a number of ways to support them in their careers—and some to avoid.

In-person support was, across the board, a huge form of support for most drag performers. "Come to see our shows and pay for tickets. That's the best way to support us, and I'm always so grateful to our audiences," said Peaches Christ. But when you attend shows, don't forget to tip. "Tipping your local queens can make a huge difference! If everyone tips, it can sometimes double our booking fees," clarified Sara Andrews.

In addition to tipping, use your voice at local clubs and venues. Creme Fatale suggested that fans "demand promoters to see us in different locations" as well as buying merchandise when it's available at shows. Buying merchandise directly from performers is important because not all retail venues share profits with queens and kings. "There are a lot of companies out there that make copies of our merchandise and throw it on their website," explained Aja. "If it's not official merchandise, it's really just taking money from the performers."

Social media is a powerful financial tool for drag performers as well. So liking and commenting on photos, videos, and original content is a big part of supporting queens and kings. "Sharing content allows us to grow and receive more bookings and paid projects," said Creme Fatale.

Last but not least, remember to support performers in your hometowns, and not just on television. "It's important for fans to continue to support their local queens and encourage their dreams," said Coco Peru. She added, "I've been fortunate to have worked in drag for twenty-seven years, long before there was a drag TV show that could catapult a career and long before there was internet that could let you reach the world. So I would just encourage fans to support their local bars, clubs, and theaters and to please keep buying tickets to our shows and not wait for 'next time.' If there is one thing I have learned in life and in business, there is nothing like 'Now's the time.'"

Last but not least, Soju made a request that was echoed by most performers: "STOP LOOKING AT YOUR PHONE WHILE WE PERFORM. Tip! Your dollar bills go a long way and most times you're watching a free show, so please tip your queens. The more love and appreciation you give us, the harder we perform! Also let a bitch know that you appreciate all the efforts they go through to put on a show for you. Do that with a five-dollar bill and you're golden." gc

FOLLOW THE QUEENS AND KINGS ONLINE:

Aja (ajakween.com)

Bob the Drag Queen (bobthedragqueen.com)

Coco Peru (misscocoperu.com)

Creme Fatale (instagram.com/cremefatale)

Heklina (instagram.com/heklina)

Peaches Christ (peacheschrist.com)

Pretty Rik E (prettyboidrag.com)

Sara Andrews (1800wigtakeout.com and instagram.com/MissSaraAndrews)

Soju (instagram.com/shotwithsoju)

Making a Statement

Designer Christian Siriano talks about taking risks, designing for women, and the evolving business of fashion.

By Fariha Roísín
Photography by the Riker Brothers

Over the last few years, Christian Siriano has been prioritizing women's bodies in an inconceivable way.

Though fashion in the recent few years or so has popped off as a pilgrimage to difference—racial diversity of models being a subject du jour—body diversity is *still* very much an underrepresented (as well as under-talked-about) faction of the conversation. We hear of famous women who aren't feeling supported by the fashion industry when it comes to wearing fashion that fits their specific body shapes, their voluptuousness, their curves—and it makes you wonder, *What really has changed?*

Leslie Jones has been very vocal in the past about designers choosing not to dress her for red-carpet events, which is a telling revelation. In a tweet while promoting her film *Ghostbusters* in 2017, she wrote: "It's so funny how there are no designers wanting to help me with a premiere dress for movie. Hmmm that will change and I remember everything." Many years ago, Christina Hendricks made a similar statement. Lest we forget, this year Cardi B rapped in "She Bad," "I could buy designer, but this Fashion Nova fit." There are still so many limitations on what designers will do and who they will dress because fashion, in many ways, is about enhancing power, and thinness is still a trope of power in the industry, as well as the world. It's also about exclusivity, and capitalism breeds on other people's feelings of insecurity. If you're not content with your own life, you're buying more to fill the void. Buying more to fit a mold that has no intention of accepting you.

But here's where Siriano comes in. His dresses have become beacons for women with curves as he has subtly shifted the paradigm of who gets to be adjacent to—and readily participate in—glamour. In the past few years, Christian has dressed Leslie Jones (in fact he replied to Leslie's aforementioned tweet with a sweet "hi" emoji) as well as Janet Mock and Christina Hendricks. Even Danielle Brooks walked down the Siriano runway, in a draping Romanesque bright teal gown, fit with a chiffon shoulder cape, hair slicked back, regal and poised, a pink-magenta (could be Fenty with its tropical pink) top lid. Brooks looked positively divine. And it's become evidently clear: Siriano knows how to cater to women who have long been left out of fashion, proving that everyone can feel good in their bodies, and be glamorous.

"I just love dressing women. I don't really care what size they are, what they look like, or where they come from," Siriano writes over email, adding, "Fashion is so powerful. We are visual creatures. We see something and it has an immediate reaction that can be good and bad . . . So I

Sometimes rejection can really push you to be even greater. If you are a fighter, which I think I am, I find that it only helps push you.

think as a designer, it's our chance to get our voice out there with our work without saying something." Fashion, for designers, is their words, is their statement.

As the youngest winner of *Project Runway* (season four, to be exact) at the ripe age of twenty-one, Siriano has experienced a lot of success in the ten years since. At the 2008 GLAAD Media Awards, Tim Gunn shared his high praise of Siriano: "I really believe he is his generation's Marc Jacobs. I really do. We have found America's next great fashion designer." High praise when, like Siriano, Jacobs had a similar fashion trajectory as the youngest designer ever to have been awarded the Council of Fashion Designers of America Perry Ellis Award for New Fashion Talent.

Siriano was born and raised in Annapolis, Maryland, and was initially inspired by his older sister and mother. "My sister was a ballet dancer and I loved being backstage with her. I really loved seeing the transformation of a dancer in sweats to then floating onstage in a tulle gown." A great metaphor for the transformation of a dress onto a body, its canvas. This early love of costuming became a motivation for design and eventually to pursue a career in fashion. "I was a very creative kid. I loved to play dress-up, I loved creating sets, and just loved clothes. It was something I just thought was interesting," he tells me, adding, "My mom and sister had great style and I think I just loved watching them get dressed." He's carried this verve and admiration with him through the years, and his love of dressing women has now evolved into a very successful business.

But the path wasn't always streamlined. After his rejection by the Fashion Institute of Technology, Siriano decided to study abroad at the American Intercontinental University in London, and shortly after started interning at Vivienne Westwood, as well as for Alexander McQueen, who Siriano claims was his favorite designer. Later, he returned to New York City, where he casually applied to compete on Bravo's one and only *Project Runway*. And, of course, the rest is, as they say, (well-documented) history. Seriously, the reruns of the episodes can still be watched on Bravo!

"Sometimes rejection can really push you to be even greater. If you are a fighter, which I think I am, I find that it only helps push you." In his own life, it really has pushed him to come full circle. Just recently FIT asked him to give their graduation speech for 2018—proof that Siriano's endurance to meet goals, no matter the roadblock, has propelled him to heights he's already surpassed. With the methodical devotion of a Scorpio, at just thirty-three years old, he's already superseded milestones that can take years to achieve, creating a business from scratch.

Siriano's drive has something to do with it, but so does his personality. He became quite the hit sensation during his tenure at *Project Runway*, mainly by garnering a bit of a reputation with his catchphrases during the season. Some of the greatest hits were: "Ferosh" (as in, ferocious), "Oh my God, I'm going to die" (like, all the time), "Fierce" (the classic Siriano choice phrase), and my favorite one-liner of all time: "I'm not a miracle worker, lady, I can't make you

have an ass!" Okay, actually, here's another one: "I love Asians. Asians are fierce!" And Amy Poehler portrayed Siriano in an episode of *Saturday Night Live*, though it doesn't quite stand the test of time. The sociopolitical landscape of America has vastly changed from 2008 to 2018, and it's *filled* to the brim with offensive, derogatory name-calling. When Janet Mock, on her podcast, asked Christian about some of these comments, especially "hot tranny mess," he explained that as a young, "exuberant" gay kid, that word (in particular) was a personal reference for him. A reference from a queer culture of his own that consisted mainly of other gay men and drag queens. So the word was normalized in that context. So, even though he never intended to hurt anyone with these comments, he had to unlearn the word from his vocabulary and now understands that the impact could be misread and could have toxic and insidious connotations, especially when transphobia was, and still is, so rampant. Trans women of color are still one of the most frequently murdered groups of women in North America.

The aesthetic of baby Siriano, back in the days of *Project Runway*, is so a part of the cultural zeitgeist of the late 2000s. Hair sideswept similar to the gelled, fang-like straight hair of Pete Wentz, punk-emo chic, with the black T-shirt and twill vest combo on lockdown. Even the profanities of that time were so specific to the advent of reality shows taking off. It was a time when we were seriously addicted to people's realness, we were addicted to their ugly, to their honesty, to their brash and wild, to the things they'd say that could make us

But being a young entrepreneur and investing time and energy in a business doesn't exist in a vacuum; it takes years of dedicated work, as well as building a team that is sustainable. "We are also competing with such large brands so we have to be just as great with less resources," Siriano adds. Building a brand from the kernel of an idea into something that has blossomed into a powerhouse is no easy feat. To be a brand that is trusted and revered is even harder. But potentially what has made Siriano stand out is his ethic to dress all kinds of women. It is exceptionally satisfying to see an actual diverse array of women's bodies decorated in fine-mesh tulle, floral-printed silks, and color so rich and bold. Most recently, he dressed writer Ashley Ford in one of the most beautiful extra-milky-coffee-colored wedding gowns. But also witness Whoopi Goldberg in a hot-pink suit with a matching billowy hat, Melissa McCarthy in a dusty rose gown with a silver brocade detail on the neckline, Patricia Clarkson in a midnight blue glitter-glam piece, or even Michelle Obama in a blue Yves Klein over-the-knee dress that she wore to her historic speech at the Democratic National Convention in support of Hillary Clinton's nomination.

"I feel like we take risks every day. It can be what looks we put on the runway, who we dress on the red carpet, et cetera. It might not always be the norm, but what is anymore?" *What is the new normal?* is a perfect question as we move forward in conversations about diversity and fashion's responsibility to the dialogue. There should be an emphasis on refusing to exaggerate things so they just become tropes, as well as a desire to resist exploiting a moment. Which is what feels so organic about Siriano's work; it's for the honest love of fashion. In many ways, he's still the young kid admiring his mother and sister, making costumes in the living room. The candid excitement is still there, and he agrees: "We just love to celebrate beauty, and that comes in so many ways." **gc**

spit out our coffee in hilarious agreement. It was as if Samantha Jones from *Sex and the City* had a soapbox, or more fittingly, a *Wendy Williams*–type talk show. We craved to know people's interiors, making reality TV one of the most lucrative endeavors of Hollywood. I mean, Siriano guest starred on *Ugly Betty* as well as made a cameo in Estelle's "No Substitute Love" music video. Both times as himself. That's a flex.

But, a decade later, change and evolution are two themes that come up in our interview a few times. "I'm always excited for change. It keeps us thinking, and pushes us to try new things," writes Siriano. These days he's more demure: His hair in a dapper cut, still dark, dark brown, but the dramatic edges are gone. Now the style is more simple-chic—blazers in cerulean blue, or black with satin panels; shirts well fitted in monochrome prints. He's back-to-basics Christian Siriano.

I ask him about his business, a fashion house he started entirely on his own, under his vision and control—an unconventional route when most designers work for, or with, other design houses before starting their own (if ever). Phoebe Philo worked at Chloé, then Céline, and though Stella McCartney launched her own fashion house in 2001, she did so in partnership with Gucci. Even Marc Jacobs, who created his own label in 1986, later went on to become creative director/vice president at Perry Ellis, then creative director at Louis Vuitton. The trajectory Siriano has taken has been unique, but speaks to his own specific vision. He knows what he wants, and he's acquiring it. "I think it's important to really stay true to yourself and follow what you believe in and can feel proud of. I have realized that the successful parts of the business are always the ones I work the hardest on and are therefore always the ones I feel the most proud of."

Should You Keep or Cut Your Day Job?

Four women talk money, work, and creativity.

By Joanna Petrone
Illustration by Louisa Bertman

Day jobs in pop culture are slogs, mere drudgery to be endured until the artist catches her big break, strikes it rich, and never looks back. In reality, the ways women navigate work, creativity, and finances are rarely that simple.

I spoke with four creatives who are making waves in their fields: Alana Massey, essayist and author of *All the Lives I Want*; Leila Weefur, multidisciplinary artist and curator for The Black Aesthetic; Jane Marie, podcast host of *The Dream* and *DTR* and owner of Little Everywhere; and Lisa Wong Jackson, graphic designer and owner of design and retail businesses Good on Paper

and Morningtide. Together, their responses paint a picture of creative success that is far more meandering, recursive, and multitudinous than what the conventional wisdom about day jobs holds. The insights they shared are far more interesting, thought-provoking, and helpful, too.

Tell me about your day job(s).

Jane Marie: Podcasting is my day job! As of last year, LOL. Before that, I was scrambling for many years, collecting different freelance contracts. This is the first time I've had a day job in seven years, and it feels wonderful. So comforting.

Leila Weefur: My day job is the audiovisual editor in chief of *Art Practical*, which is one of the only art publications in the Bay Area.

Lisa Wong Jackson: I recently left my design job at an engineering/architecture firm after nearly twenty years. I am a freelance graphic designer for my own company called Good on Paper as well as co-owner of a small lifestyle shop in Albany, California, called Morningtide.

Alana Massey: When I was working day jobs and routinely failing to stay in any one of them for any respectable amount

Left to Right: Leila Weefur, Jane Marie,
Lisa Wong Jackson & Alana Massey

of time that could be put on a résumé as anything more than a red flag, I was constantly in awe of the statistical improbability that I kept delightedly getting hired for what I would quickly come to see were actually such bad jobs. Looking back, the single common denominator was that I was really excellent at getting hired for jobs and really terrible at actually having one. And I don't mean like some stifled artist who refuses to be tethered to a screen for eight hours, I mean that it was my fault that I was bored and disorganized and only productive at strange hours and long intervals that I couldn't predict and that likely made me very difficult to work with and to manage. I had short stints mostly in the nonprofit world, first in a few administrative roles and later working in nonprofit public relations, but the most consistent day job I had before writing full-time was doing sex work, mostly independently by carving out my own niche. Even when I was working in strip clubs with a schedule every week, I was classified as an independent contractor and had minimal daily instruction from management besides "Go make money." These days, I don't have a manager to make the order, so I write to-do lists in the first person, each task starting with "I will . . ."

Approximately what percentage of your income comes from your creative work and what percentage comes from your day job(s)? How has this changed over time?

Jane Marie: Now it's 100 percent, which is wonderful and something I've yearned for for a long time. The problem with creative work is that you need time. Not time to actually be creating, but time *not doing anything* for your brain to breathe and for breakthroughs. When I've had a stressful day job, I've always felt guilty for even thinking that. Like, how could I ever justify the hours or days of staring at a wall that come with being a writer? It's balanced by intense nights and weekends and never really being off the clock as a business owner, so I no longer worry about it.

Leila Weefur: I think it actually always changes over time, meaning that it fluctuates. Right now, a large part of my income comes from my day job. It's actually the most balanced it's ever been, close to fifty-fifty, because I'm just doing *Art Practical*. But there are times when I teach, so I have less time for my art practice, which makes it more of an eighty-twenty or seventy-thirty, which is kind of the usual.

Lisa Wong Jackson: When I had a regular day job, about 80 percent of my income was from my day job, and 20 percent from my creative work. Now that I've left my day job, all of my income comes from Good on Paper and Morningtide.

Alana Massey: I am always afraid to answer this type of question because the concept of "creative work" is one I really struggle with, because I do not want to be pedantic or aloof toward creative processes, but I think we mistakenly classify work as creative if the end product is one of a fairly narrow selection of what we consider "creations": a painting, a story, a wool scarf, an out-of-the-box logo, a dining table centerpiece made from an unexpected textile you have lying around, et cetera. This designation disguises how much non-creative labor goes into any end product that does fit within these narrow criteria, and it also doesn't honor how much creative work goes into jobs that we don't even take the time to summarily dismiss as uncreative because it never occurs to us. *So,* 100 percent of my income comes from writing, and this has been the case since 2015. My end products are books, essays, reported features, op-eds, reviews, blog posts, product descriptions, web copy, brand taglines, and even the occasional long-form luxury Instagram caption. And I never know on any given day or any project how the work will be divided across research, collaboration, placement strategy that takes into account timing, outlet prestige

> *"As a creative, that [time off] is one of the most valuable times because that is when we are opening ourselves up to new ideas and daydreaming and imagining." —Leila Weefur*

versus visibility, monetary self-interest, principled self-interest, et cetera. Mostly I just wish I had more time in the day for making fan videos about my friends and their cats, and sitting down with my new hobby of rendering intergalactic dreamscapes in middle-school-style collages by cutting up my backlog of *Vogue*s, *National Geographic*s, *Allure*s, *Real Simple*s, and a smattering of poems and cartoons from *The New Yorker*.

What lessons, skills, or interests have you picked up from your day job(s) that carry over to your creative work?

Jane Marie: I started out in the service industry as a grocery bagger before working in bars and restaurants for a number of years. I think those customer-focused roles really taught me how to talk to strangers, which is the number one skill you need in being a reporter. They also taught me to show up on time and not be a jerk! And freelancing helped me become a business owner because it's essentially like running a small business with all the bookkeeping and whatnot. If I hadn't been forced to get used to doing that stuff daily, we'd never have gotten through our first year.

Leila Weefur: In my day job, I have to be highly communicative. Part of my job is managing a team of people—podcast

hosts, freelance audio editors, audio producer—and I think that that has sharpened my skills at communicating efficiently and structuring my time. Time management has become really important when you are juggling so many things. On any given week, I have to give a lecture two days a week, then I have to install a show, then I have a one-off event, and then on top of that we have staff meetings on Monday, and the rest of the week is remote, so I have to very cautiously and considerately structure my time so I can best serve my team and myself—and so I don't let my art practice drop. Time management is everything.

Lisa Wong Jackson: Oftentimes at my day job, I would have to work within a very tight time frame, which was sometimes challenging, but I've learned to manage my time better because of it.

Can you talk about the relationship between money and creativity that exists for you, personally?

Jane Marie: I have poor-kid brain and I never won't have poor-kid brain, so money plays a really interesting role in my creativity. There's a lot of rules ingrained in me about money and "goodness." Too much and you are greedy. Not enough and you're lazy. So slide an interest in creative work in there and things can get really messy,

really stressful on a daily basis. I've had to teach myself that it's okay to, say, stare at that wall when I can't figure out where to go with a story. My gut instinct is, "If there's time to lean, there's time to clean," and I try to stick to that but I also try to cut myself some slack. I've also had to learn the value in appreciating creativity out in the world as part of my practice. It's actually part of my job to read books and go to movies and museums. I think my younger self would've scoffed at me taking any time for that, but I get it now how much that unpaid work pays you in the end.

Leila Weefur: I think as an artist there's pressure to make sure your income comes from selling work, but I've been pretty intentional in making sure that I have a practice that isn't centered around selling my work. So I don't sell my work—anytime I show it in a gallery space, I usually don't sell it. I'm not usually hanging 2-D work. I do make other printed matter like zines or chapbooks, and, as of late, I've been giving them away at my openings because I feel like art should be made in the spirit of generosity. If there's always underlying pressure to sell something or for someone to buy something, that means that you are looking at your work as though it were a product, and for me, creativity in my art practice is not about making a product. You'll never see any price tags or a list of prices for my

> *"I have redefined success in a way that's helped me slow down, be more mindful, and invest in fewer but better things." —Lisa Wong Jackson*

work anywhere. I will sell to a collection, museum, or library because I feel that is serving a greater institutional purpose. I do apply to grants; I just got the first grant I've ever applied to, the Creative Work Fund Grant, and I'm learning how to structure my words so that not only can I pay myself for the work that I do but I can pay the people who are also working with me. I always want my work, whether it is my personal practice or it is The Black Aesthetic, to be in a generous space, in an ecosystem where it feeds everyone, potentially.

Lisa Wong Jackson: The financial stability I had when I had my day job definitely allowed me to take more creative risks and pursue the projects I wanted, as well as say no to ones that weren't the right fit. Now that I've left my day job, however, there is a bit more pressure financially, but I am also a lot happier, which results in better work for my clients and for our shop.

Alana Massey: There's an iconic exchange in the teen comedy *10 Things I Hate About You* where the two sisters, Bianca and Kat, in one of the many scenes where their overbearing dad's interferences in their lives turns into the two girls bickering. Bianca, the younger and sweeter sister, sneers, "Where did you come from? Planet 'Loser'?" to which Kat, an admittedly principled feminist who mistakes surliness for

a revolutionary virtue unto itself, replies, "As opposed to Planet 'Look at Me, Look at Me'?" making exaggerated hand gestures and speaking in the laziest of ditzy voice impressions that sounds nothing like her sister. Since I first saw that movie when I was thirteen years old, I have known and been comfortable with the fact that I am a proud and loyal citizen of Planet Look at Me, Look at Me. I don't know how a Protestant ethic that one's work should always be useful to others or to some greater good got lodged into my identity, but I've never minded it half as much as other people have. Even in my childhood diaries, I can see how I'm writing for an imagined audience, I see my own silences and my embellishments of the moral instruction learned from another Thursday in the seventh grade. I want my writing to make people feel seen, sometimes in ways that draw them out of invisibility, and sometimes that draws them into acknowledging their own complicity in a harm to which they must hold themselves accountable. I think that my greatest creative gift is in making my perspective widely legible and sufficiently generous to reach a lot of readers without compromising the integrity or diminishing the stakes of the topic at hand.

How do you manage your time and energy so that you can pursue your creative work without burning out?

Jane Marie: What is this "not burning out" you speak of? I haven't been able to avoid that so far in any of my creative pursuits. It's something I need to work on.

Leila Weefur: I have started using project-management software, lots of calendar alerts, and making sure I schedule time when I know I can't take any other meetings. I dedicate that time just to do my day job or I dedicate that time just to be in the studio. I dedicate Tuesdays for my self-care. I'm a big proponent of therapy and acupuncture. Making sure you schedule a day to have a day off so you have time for yourself, just to lie in bed, is really important to not burning out. As a creative, that is one of the most valuable times because that is when we are opening ourselves up to new ideas and daydreaming and imagining.

Lisa Wong Jackson: I make to-do lists and love crossing them off! Sticking to a routine helps a lot, too. Between all the kids' stuff, a new puppy, freelance projects, and working at Morningtide, I get work done on the days I'm not at the shop as well as at night after the kids are in bed. I've been trying to pace myself so that I'm not on the computer too late. And a couple of times a week I take a group Pilates reformer class called Bodyrok that kicks my ass and gives me strength and energy to keep going.

Alana Massey: I don't manage either and I burn out constantly.

In a society that often defines success in terms of money and what money can buy, how do you measure the success of your creative work when that worth is not necessarily reflected in the marketplace?

Jane Marie: For better or worse, my creative endeavors started in a field and at a time where we didn't really get paid in dollars. I was blogging and making videos, so I had to get my pay through positive feedback. Unfortunately, that training has led me to devalue some of my work, I think. Like in terms of dollars. If anything, my problem is feeling like I deserve even one dollar for doing what I do. So, I know I'm successful, but it has literally nothing to do with what's in the bank.

Leila Weefur: I measure the success based on the conversations I have with people. There are tons of ways for success to be measured in creative work when it is not reflected in the marketplace, but you have to first decide: What success are you trying to achieve? My personal success meter is: Is my visual practice, is my visual aesthetic, getting better? Is it reflective of itself? Is it considering itself? Am I growing? Am I able to spend time reading and writing?

Am I contributing to my personal growth and is that then contributing to the larger conversation about race and about the Black body and about how the Black body is negotiating itself within the world of language and interaction? I think as long as people are receptive to the work and are wanting and giving me ways to continue the conversation, then I think the work is successful.

Lisa Wong Jackson: Leaving my day job has actually forced me to really think about money in a way I didn't have to as much before. The freelance life can be unstable with clients not paying on time, et cetera—oh, how I miss those regular paychecks! But I wouldn't trade it for anything because ultimately my well-being and happiness are what matters most as it makes me a better mother, wife, friend, and caretaker. I have redefined success in a way that's helped me slow down, be more mindful, and invest in fewer but better things.

Alana Massey: The marketplace's very existence is contingent on it undervaluing all work and yet still being relied upon to measure work's worth. I have never really looked at a book or painting or screenplay and felt confident that I could be in even a ballpark range of its actual value, and so when I've negotiated higher rates and

been able to develop a roster of outlets and brands that pay a certain rate, it has been more about the practicality and the principle of feeling entitled to living wages. And more and more, I find the most challenging and imperative creative project of our time is developing modes of being in solidarity with people from across a huge range of industries and regions and identities to create actual systemic change. Workers are adding record amounts of value to the marketplace and getting a pittance back. Something I've been doing a lot of lately is listening and looking for languages and ways of communicating a story or idea where I hadn't seen them before. What started as a short sojourn down a poetry rabbit hole ended up with me spending weeks trying to understand Alan Turing's work and training in crisis-intervention models that don't involve cops or hospitals. The measure of my success isn't going to be found in work I've already been paid for, but in how expansive my list of future inquiries into all of the curious and incredible ways people create and communicate the world. **gc**

12 things i wish i knew before I started FREE-LANCING full-time

From self-care to tax breaks, freelance rules of thumb to follow for a smoother transition.

By Nikki Carter
Illustrated by Celeste Prevost
Lettering by Erin Ellis

I've been running a side hustle as a writer and editor since 2011, but it wasn't until this year that I finally made the long-awaited leap to supporting myself solely through contract work. I'd saved up enough to support myself for about six months if my business wasn't pulling in enough income, and I was moving temporarily to Northern California—so it wasn't like I'd be building a long-term career there, anyway. The timing of it all felt serendipitous.

It was high time for the change, but it was also incredibly scary and unpredictable. There were many roadblocks I ran into when it came to managing my time, money, and personal development—and as I've talked with other freelancers, I've found that I'm far from alone in facing these struggles.

As I write this, I'm wholly affirmed in my decision to leave the security of a steady paycheck, benefits, and paid time off to invest in and grow my business. I now work about 30 to 40 percent of the hours I put in during my previous corporate life, yet I make just as much, and sometimes more, than I used to. I'm grateful for this life I'm carving out on my own terms and in which, despite the challenges, there are many upsides. As one of my first major clients put it, "Entrepreneurship is hard as hell, but the view from the top is breathtaking."

If you're on this journey, whether you're a seasoned business owner or just dipping your toes in the water, I applaud you. It takes courage to put your neck on the line and follow this path, and persistence to stay committed when things get tough or uncertain. In the spirit of support and collaboration, I'd like to share some of the major things I wish I'd known before I dove headfirst into full-time freelancing. I hope one or more of these helps to smooth your learning curve.

1. Be specific about your goals.

Setting clear and specific goals will help guide you toward the right decisions as you start to grow your business.

2. Schedule your time and hold yourself accountable, just as you would with a traditional employer.

This one is tough, and I'm still working at it every day. So far, I've experimented with a couple different ways of managing my time. My first attempt involved sitting down, writing down everything I wanted to accomplish over the course of a week (billable client work, pitching articles, going on hikes, fitting in time to talk with friends and family, et cetera). Then, I figured out how many hours I would allocate for each activity on a given day.

While it seemed promising initially, the execution of this plan went terribly. My proposed schedule looked something like this:

8–9 a.m.: Meditation, exercise
9–10 a.m.: Search and apply for new jobs/projects
10–1: Current client work/projects
1–3: Write, work on personal writing goals
3–5: Business/personal development time—reading blogs, listening to podcasts, figuring out ways to improve
5–6: Catch up with friends and family

Looking back, I don't know *how* I thought this was a good idea, but I can tell you that trying to spread my energy across so many different things for short bursts of time just did not work for me—at all. I felt scattered, frenzied, and ineffective. What has worked much better is to set aside *longer* blocks of time—or even days—to focus on a project or task. It takes me a while to get in the groove, so once I'm in the zone, I can take advantage of it by remaining there for a longer period of time.

It may take a few botched experiments before you find the system that best optimizes your time. **Don't beat yourself up about it—this is all part of the journey. Once you've figured out how you'll schedule your time, the next step is to keep holding yourself accountable.** Treat showing up for work as you would any other job. If possible, section off a dedicated space where you can comfortably work, or consider joining a co-working collective.

Now, when I sit down at my desk each weekday morning, my body and mind have an almost Pavlovian response—they know it's business time.

3. If you're just starting out, consider taking on volunteer projects.

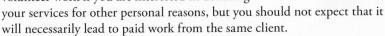

There is absolutely nothing wrong with taking on unpaid work if you're new to the game and looking to gain relevant experience. However, I don't recommend working for free as a long-term strategy to grow your business. There is value in volunteer work if you are interested in donating your services for other personal reasons, but you should not expect that it will necessarily lead to paid work from the same client.

The point of serving in a pro bono capacity is to give you experience to point to on your résumé, on LinkedIn, and during interviews. If you know you're a solid writer, designer, or other creative but don't have anything to show off in your portfolio, that can be a really tough sell for a client. Volunteer work shows you have the skills while serving as evidence of your work quality.

Ultimately, through volunteering I've gotten some really helpful references, gained confidence in areas I wasn't particularly skilled in, and expanded my network.

5. Yes, your brand is a business, but that doesn't mean you need to hide your true personality.

Tuning in to who you really are and who you want to work with most is crucial. Especially if you're coming from a traditional business environment, you may be tempted to put on a buttoned-up persona in order to do business. I promise you that this is not an approach that will lead to happiness. The *real* you is what will attract the type of clients you'll work best with because they're attracted to your personality and style.

For me, it's women, and in particular, women of color, whom I want to support most. My "Services" page on my website is written in my own tone and highlights my interests and strengths in a way that I think will speak to my target audience. If someone is completely turned off by my style or tone, that's okay, because we wouldn't have been a good fit anyway.

4. Interview smarter, not harder.

I've told everyone I love about this already, so consider yourself part of my inner circle now: One trick I've come to rely on is using what I call my "interview cheat sheet." This handy document is saved on my computer and outlines my rates at the top, as well as categories of my experience throughout the rest of the page.

I broke my work history into buckets like "Editing," "Blogs," and "Content Strategy," and then listed anything I'd done that pertained to those skills. If there were quantifiable metrics associated with that work, I listed those, too. I also added a section that covers what industries my clients are in, as well as which projects I've enjoyed the most.

It could also be worthwhile to add some personal reminders to this document. If you work best in a collaborative environment, make a note of that to remind yourself not to accept positions that will be more isolating and independent. If you require regular check-ins to feel like you're on track, that's worth bringing up so you and a potential client are on the same page.

I used to feel so clumsy and awkward as I searched for answers to various questions during an interview. Now I just pull up my cheat sheet before the call so I can quickly cite any relevant experience, what type of client I did it for, and anything else the interviewer wants to know. I sound much more focused, polished, and aware. I can't recommend doing this enough.

6. There's no real magic formula for setting rates, but you need to account for factors beyond just your time.

There are many resources out there to help you set your rates, so I won't dive into formulas here. What I will say is that you should remember you'll need a cushion to account for administrative time—answering emails, responding to texts, answering Slack messages, and the like. Freelancing can often mean we're always available to clients, and you likely won't remember to bill for that two-minute text session you had earlier this morning.

To remedy this, consider adding a small-percentage "administrative fee" cushion to your rates. This will help you feel better about the time you spend thinking about ideas for clients when you're technically "off the clock" or taking phone calls and texts from them as needed. Also, be sure to build in a buffer for taxes and the other expenses you need to account

for as a self-employed business owner. It can be exciting to get an offer from a client for more than you're used to making, but you have to remember that you'll now be paying your own taxes, healthcare premiums, and other bills you may not be used to. After you deduct those costs, is the offer still exciting to you?

Last, if you find yourself charging different clients different rates, don't fret. This is totally normal. I consider projects on a case-by-case basis and as a result, I have clients who pay me on the higher and lower end of the spectrum. As an example: Though I have set rates, if a client has a lot of work to offer me or can agree to an ongoing retainer, I'll consider lowering my hourly rate, because it's worth it in the end.

8. Likewise, don't be intimidated by increasing your rates for existing clients.

Inflation happens across all categories. You aren't alone if you're thinking about raising your rates, and you aren't wrong for doing so. That said, you'll need to be thoughtful when approaching this conversation with clients you want to retain. Every situation is different, but the fact is that the client needs to understand how this benefits *them*, so you don't want to only point to the value that a higher rate will bring *you*.

Does this higher rate mean that you can now prioritize a long-term relationship with your client? Does it mean that you'll be able to guarantee a quicker turnaround time than the one they are used to? Whatever benefit will be passed on to the client should be clearly illuminated in your proposal to raise rates.

Be open to negotiation, too. Your client may have been wanting to ask for something different, too, and this is the perfect time to discuss it.

The bottom line is that there's no harm in asking, and there may actually be harm in *not*. You will only grow to resent clients that you believe aren't paying what you're worth. Always remember that unknown rates can't be met!

7. Know your worth, and don't be afraid to ask for it.

There are a ton of freelancers out there, and that can make it really hard to stick to your guns when it comes to the minimum rate you'll accept. I know a lot of people succumb to the bidding wars that take place for freelance work but unless you're just starting out, I think it's a good practice to value your work product enough to stand by your rates.

What if you believed that for every client who can't meet your rate, there is another out there who can—and will? Searching and landing these clients may take effort, but you'll be a *lot* happier come invoice day if you're getting paid a rate that respects your time.

I AM WORTH IT

A Few Rules of Thumb

a. Having at least three, if not more, months of living expenses in a savings account is ideal. Client work can be volatile and you don't want to be caught off guard by a period with low income and no savings. After I left my full-time job, I ended up pulling from my savings accounts for several months before my business was truly stable. I know people who have saved for *years* before taking the leap so they didn't have to worry about financial security on top of building their business.

b. Don't neglect your retirement accounts. After you build up your savings, directing a steady stream of money toward retirement should be your next priority.

c. Keep tabs on how much money you're bringing in, as well as where your money is going. I maintain a spreadsheet that outlines my clients, how many hours I typically work for them, and how much revenue I can count on in a typical month. It also lists my fixed expenses, like rent and insurance, and estimates for variable costs like gas and food. This way, if I lose a specific client, I can go into the spreadsheet and see exactly how that affects my bottom line—do I need to pitch another client? Can I reduce one of my variable expenses to adjust?

Money is already such a sensitive and stressful topic that many of us tend to avoid getting clear about the financial state we're in, but you *have* to work through that if you want to be a successful freelancer.

9. Taxes and healthcare are no longer a given—you, and only you, are responsible for these now.

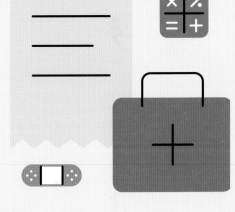

As a contractor, you are responsible for paying estimated quarterly taxes to the IRS, as well as carrying your own health insurance. I like to pay my taxes on a monthly basis—when all my invoices are paid, I submit roughly 26 percent to the IRS and then I don't think about it for another month. This helps me avoid overspending because when I look at my bank account, I know that the money in there is actually mine.

Look into tax breaks that you're eligible for, as well as how this year's tax changes affect you going forward, and keep detailed records so that your life isn't a circus come tax time. There are lots of tax breaks for self-employed folks: You can write off fees you have to pay via PayPal or WePay transactions, site hosting fees, your dedicated office space, health-insurance premiums, advertising, any equipment you need to do your job (hello, here's the excuse you've been waiting for to upgrade your dusty old laptop!), and more.

When tax season does roll around, consider hiring an accountant or CPA who has worked with contractors before; they may be able to highlight savings you weren't aware of.

10. Set savings goals and get to squirreling.

Without an employer match to your 401(k), paid time off, and some of the other benefits of working for a traditional employer, you'll have to figure out how to take care of your future financial security yourself.

11. Scheduled time off is mandatory to preserve your sanity.

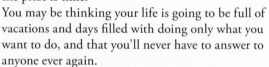

As my best friend, Colleen, puts it, "Freelance doesn't mean free time like I thought it did." Amen, sister! Leaving a job that provided you a set schedule and clear expectations in order to work for yourself can feel like you won a lottery in which the prize is time. You may be thinking your life is going to be full of vacations and days filled with doing only what you want to do, and that you'll never have to answer to anyone ever again.

The truth is that while this lifestyle is amazing and offers a degree of flexibility many others don't, you will probably find that once you are solely responsible for your own success, you can't stop thinking about work. It's hard to turn it off! If you're a motivated, driven person like many successful freelancers tend to be, you might feel tempted to always be "on," thinking about ideas, being accessible to clients for questions, producing content.

This can be especially challenging if you work from home and don't have any physical boundaries separating you from your work. I'm gonna cut it to you straight: *Time off is not negotiable.* Be very clear with yourself, because you will try to wriggle out of this time and again. You will find yourself on vacation, trying to schedule blocks of time to work early in the morning before your trip mates are awake. You will feel guilty every time you try to relax and read a book, because you could be working and making money instead.

Find time to truly unplug. Get off the grid. Taking time away from work is good for your health and it actually benefits your business: You will gain inspiration, insights, and energy that will make you ultimately better at your craft and more valuable to clients.

Now, I will say that being out of the office will take some extra planning that you may not be used to. You'll need to let clients know when you'll be gone, *how* gone you'll be (e.g., if you'll be checking email occasionally, every day, or not at all), and how this affects your work for them. Are you having someone else take over temporarily? Are you working more before your trip so they can rest assured everything is taken care of?

Be transparent with your clients about how things will be while you're out of the office. Then when the time comes for your trip, you can enjoy it knowing that you've planned ahead and everyone is comfortable.

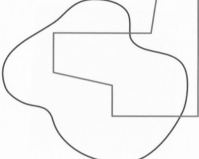

12. Finally, set firm boundaries with clients.

This goes hand in hand with the point above. Don't be afraid to communicate your limits and expectations to clients. If you don't work weekends, say so. If you straight-up don't function before 8 a.m., let them know.

When it comes to my own boundary setting, I've struggled with enforcing reasonable turnaround times. My tendency is to want to deliver things quickly—even if I get them on short, or no, notice. It took a friend with a lot of freelance experience to remind me that I'm not doing myself any favors by letting clients think they can rush in last-minute and I'll always be there. I've started asking for a two-to seven-day window to finish things, depending on the complexity of the project, and I'm now able to manage multiple projects more easily.

I have found that doing a good job while you *are* on the clock and producing deliverables on deadline (as well as being completely honest when an on-time delivery is not possible) leads clients to trust you and your work and as a result, they will respect and appreciate your boundaries.

I truly hope these tips have been helpful to you in some way, and I would love to hear about any tips you have! Good luck in all of your personal and professional endeavors, and may we always strive to support each other along the way. gc

How Will You Increase Profit as a Small Company?

The answer isn't as simple as working more hours. You have to remember that you only contain so much creative brainpower and work capacity each day. If you find yourself needing to bill more hours but don't feel you have the creative bandwidth to support it, try pinpointing ancillary services you can offer. In other words, are there things you can do that still speak to your strengths without completely exhausting you?

For example, I find that I can only write in a focused way or do strategy work for a few hours each morning, but I can also spend the afternoon editing, proofing, or doing social media tasks without completely taxing my brain. Those tasks don't require as much mental processing and allow me to keep billing, even after my "creative sprint" is over for the day.

If you're new to goal setting and unsure of how to get started, read up on how to create a strategic marketing plan for your business. Considering your business from various angles and diving deep to answer the questions it takes to put together such a plan will help you greatly.

Your goals should be the guideposts that direct and inform all of your future choices. For example, a primary goal for me when I started freelancing was to use the extra flexibility to publish more of my own writing—like this piece! Reminding myself of my big-picture goals is helpful when I'm tempted to, say, take on a new client because I have a few extra hours to spare.

INFO BOX
Job Searching/Networking

Here are some resources I like for finding jobs in writing/editing/content strategy, although some of these feature a range of contract opportunities:

Mediabistro: mediabistro.com

Remotive: remotive.io

AngelList: angel.co

CloudPeeps: cloudpeeps.com

BloggingPro: bloggingpro.com/jobs

There's an option to "search all of Craigslist." This can be helpful to find remote jobs or jobs that use specific keywords. Indeed searches using the same keywords.

(Note: These keywords should also be sprinkled throughout your résumé in case companies are searching for candidates that way.)

Facebook groups have been incredibly valuable to me when it comes to finding work and making connections. There are networking groups for many niches, so ask around within your industry to find out about them and/or be added to them.

(Note: I must acknowledge here the spaces of privilege I occupy that lend themselves well to being heard. I am a sometimes-white-passing, able-bodied woman with an advanced degree and access to familial financial support. I understand that we are all coming from different backgrounds and facing different challenges.)

how to negotiate SALARY or PAY

A step-by-step guide to knowing, asking for, and getting what you need at work.

By Kathlyn Hart
Lettering by Erin Ellis

PREPARE

1. Identify Your Worth

Being successful in any negotiation starts with understanding your unique strengths and what you bring to the table. Take the time to think through the strengths, skills, and experiences that you have.

2. Understand the Scope

In order to be able to come up with a reasonable number, you first need to understand what your job will entail.

3. Research Fair-Market Rates

Once you know the scope of the work, you can begin doing research to understand how much it should cost. Use online resources as well as your network.

4. Create Your "Wish, Want, Walk" Numbers

Based on your research and understanding of the skills, strengths, and experience you bring to the table, you can create your "wish, want, walk" numbers.

5. Up Your Expectations

So often we may come up with "wish, want, walk" numbers that feel safe. In a negotiation we will often start high and come down, so don't sell yourself short. Allow yourself to up your expectations of what you desire.

PLAN

6. Understand Clients' Needs

Often we can feel grateful to have a work opportunity open up to us, but the reality is, clients have needs that we are fulfilling. The more we can understand their needs and pain points, the better we can position ourselves in the negotiation.

7. Adopt a "Win-Win" Mind-set

Negotiation can feel like a gross, icky thing. However, at the end of the day it's just a conversation where two people come to an agreement. Women are amazing negotiators when it comes to our loved ones. Adopt a win-win mind-set and you'll see that we are just trying to make sure both sides are happy.

8. Prepare for Pushback

The more you can prepare for phrases such as "Unfortunately that's as high as we can go," the better. Think of the phrases they might say and . . .

9. Visualize Your Success

Nerves can run at an all-time high as soon as the negotiation conversation begins. Practice visualizing your success ahead of time. How will you look walking into the room, what will their reaction be, how will you respond if they object, how will you steer the conversation in a direction where you both win?

10. Schedule Your Meeting

You've prepared and practiced enough and now it's time to schedule the meeting. Vocal tone and silence are super important in conveying your emotions and understanding theirs, so set up a time to either meet in person or talk over the phone.

PITCH

11. State Your Desired Rate

Show gratitude and then succinctly state your ask starting with your "wish" number, looping in your "badassity."

For example: "Hi, _____ , thank you so much for meeting with me today. I'm extremely excited for the opportunity to work with you as a _____ . I wanted to connect with you to see if there is flexibility in the salary. Based on _____ [looping in your skills, strengths, experience, and accomplishments], I was wondering if we could explore a starting rate of _____ ."

12. Embrace Silence

After stating your desired salary, the most important thing to do is zip it. It will feel awkward, uncomfortable, and ten seconds will feel like ten minutes, but it is critical. Remember that a negotiation is a conversation, so allow the other party to respond.

13. Focus on Facts, Not Feelings

In response you will likely get pushback. Although you have prepared what to say (or not say), emotions will be at an all-time high. Take a deep breath before responding and keep your attention on the facts regarding market rate, rather than your feelings.

14. Look for Ways to Expand the Pie

There may be times when salary isn't going to be something you can both come to a final agreement on. In that case look for alternative ways that you both can compromise. Can there be flexibility in the timeline? How many hours are expected? Are there additional perks they can throw in?

15. Decide When to Flex and When to Walk Away

Ideally you will be able to find a compromise between your "wish" and "want" numbers. However, sometimes we are only able to negotiate closer to our "walk" number. At this point you will need to decide whether you want to flex or walk away. Remember that your time is just as valuable as theirs. If this isn't the right opportunity at the moment, it is perfectly acceptable to say thank you and that you would love to reconnect in the future. **gc**

how to save for RETIREMENT

Saving for something that won't happen for another forty years may not seem like a priority, but that time goes fast and your investments will have more time to grow if you start ASAP. There are plenty of options for starting a retirement fund that require minimal effort, regardless of how much money you bring in each month. You don't need to understand the stock market or world economics to start preparing for the day you can finally stop hustling.

I haven't had a full-time job for the past two years, which effectively means my retirement savings came to a screeching halt. Going freelance typically comes with new challenges—How am I going to find work? What if I don't get paid on time? Should I put on pants today?—and, frankly, saving for something that won't happen for another forty years didn't seem like a priority.

I'm not alone in putting this responsibility off. Two-thirds of working millennials between the ages of twenty-one and thirty-two don't have anything saved for retirement, according to a 2018 report from the National Institute on Retirement Security. Of course, there's more to the story than young people simply not knowing how to save; debt plays a major role in why 81 percent of freelancers of all ages can't afford to save for retirement, according to a 2018 study on the gig economy by the online investment company Betterment.

There's no specific time you should start saving for retirement, and everyone's specific financial situations are different. But Nick Holeman, a senior financial planner at Betterment, says, "The earlier the better."

Before you jump in, though, there are two things you should get under control: your debt and your emergency fund. It's generally best to work toward paying off any high-interest debt before you start a retirement fund. Holeman classifies this as any debt with an interest rate higher than 6 or 7 percent, because it's unlikely you would make more money through investments than you'll lose paying off the interest. As for debt with lower interest rates, just make sure you can swing the monthly payments before starting to save for other goals.

It's also important to build up an emergency fund before putting money toward retirement—especially for freelancers. It's widely recommended that everyone save enough money to cover between three and six months' worth of living expenses in case you lose your job, have a medical emergency, or have any other unforeseen circumstances pop up. This fund should be more like six to nine months' worth of expenses for freelancers, according to Holeman, since work can be more sporadic and paychecks often arrive at a snail's pace.

Once you have your high-interest debt in check and a healthy sum in your bank account, you're ready to start saving for retirement. Here's what to keep in mind.

First Things First: Open an Account
Sounds easy enough, but where to start? Before you kick yourself for choosing a career path that requires you to take care of this without the help of an employer, know that there's an upside to starting your own retirement fund.

"A lot of 401(k)s out there are not very transparent. They have a very limited set or very poor investment choices, and they have really high fees as well," Holeman said. "So one of the benefits of being a freelancer is that you're not stuck with the 401(k) plan that your employer happens to use."

When it comes to choosing which type of account works best for you, IRAs offer tax benefits that other types of accounts don't. A traditional IRA offers an immediate tax break by allowing you to only pay taxes on its contents when you withdraw the money. With a Roth IRA, retirement funds are taxed up front rather than when you withdraw the money in retirement.

For younger people, paying taxes now through a Roth IRA can save money in the long run, says Catherine Collinson, CEO and president of the nonprofit Transamerica Center for Retirement Studies. You end up paying taxes on your income when it's relatively low rather than paying taxes on a chunk of retirement funds that has been growing for forty years. A traditional IRA can be more predictable, however, since no one knows what tax rates will look like decades from now.

The other thing to keep in mind when deciding what account to open is what

(without a lot of money)

By Lauren Holter
Lettering by Erin Ellis

type of fees you'll be charged. Different financial institutions charge different fees for IRAs, so be cognizant of what the account you sign up for really entails.

"If you're not able to afford to save that much—maybe you're just barely tucking away a little bit of money every month— then you want to make sure that money is working as hard as possible for you," Holeman says.

Making sure your account fees are as low as possible is a good place to start.

Figure Out Your Ideal Savings

Regardless of how much money you make, it's important to sit down and plan how much you want to save each month. Holeman recommends what he calls "backwards budgeting," which simply means contributing to your retirement fund right when you get paid and then spending the rest of your money however you want.

It's also helpful to decide how much you would contribute each month in an ideal world, even if you don't have the means yet. If you know what amount you want to save each month, you can start working toward that goal. After all, it's difficult to know whether your monthly payments actually put you on track for retirement without planning ahead.

Keep your taxes in mind, too. A little-known tax benefit called the Saver's Credit offers single people making less than

$31,500 a year a tax break in return for contributing to retirement.

Decide on a Payment Method

Of course, the best way to make sure you save money every month is to set up automatic payments. But that can be tricky when you don't make the same amount every month and often find yourself chasing down invoices. It might work better to set a reminder on your phone to contribute to retirement on the same day every month, even if you can't deposit the same amount each time.

Or you can turn to an app to simplify the process. Investment platforms all offer different features, but Betterment has a SmartDeposit payment method that saves your extra cash. Rather than setting a fixed amount to contribute to retirement each month, you set how much cash you want to keep in your bank account and SmartDeposit puts anything that exceeds that amount into your retirement fund.

It's all about figuring out what works best for you.

Consider a Mid-Risk Plan for Investments

"A lot of millennials are not investing aggressively enough in their retirement accounts," Holeman says. "They have too much in cash or low-risk investments."

At the same time, though, he warns against taking too big of a risk and putting all your eggs in one basket. Financial

planners recommend investing in a diverse set of stocks and bonds to ensure that your money will perform well over the next few decades.

If you go with an automated investment service firm such as Wealthfront, you don't have to worry too much about an investment plan, as it will take care of everything for you. But if you want to be in control of your investments, be sure to do your homework. And don't be afraid to seek help from a professional financial planner.

You worked hard for that money—make sure it's working hard for you. **gc**

Apps to Help Make Saving Pain-Free

 Betterment: For people who want technology to take the lead but also prefer the security of having human advisors on standby.

 Wealthfront: For people who want computers to do most of the work and have at least $500 to start an account.

 Mint: For people who want to stay on top of bills and their budget and save for retirement all in one place.

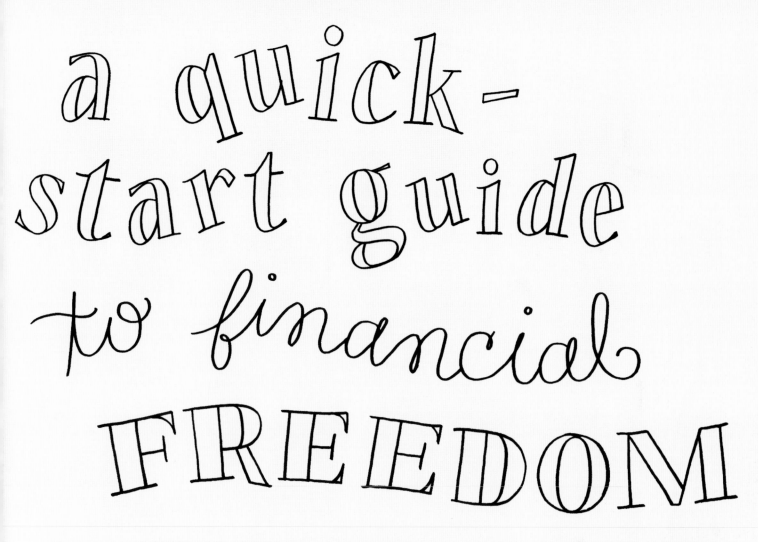

a quick-start guide to financial FREEDOM

Six steps to help you navigate and create long-term (and meaningful) financial stability.

By Jamila Souffrant
Photography by Heather Sten
Lettering by Erin Ellis

About five years ago, I was pregnant with my first son, stuck in a four-hour commute driving home from a job that I didn't love. Although I was making a good salary, I felt stuck and unhappy. It was the wake-up call that I needed to find a different way of life. After having a breakdown in my car and to my husband when I got home, I vowed that I would figure a way out of the rat race.

I started to listen to a lot of personal-finance podcasts and read blogs on my commute and in my spare time. That's when I found out about something called the FIRE (financial independence, retire early) movement. Everyday people were able to optimize their finances and reach a point where working for money became optional. The concept of financial independence appealed to me because it was

what I was searching for most of my life—the ability to do what I wanted, spend time with the people I loved, and enjoy life without having to worry about money.

While I was inspired by other people's stories on podcasts and blogs, I couldn't always relate to them. Raised by a single mom who immigrated here from the island of Jamaica, I yearned to see more people who looked and sounded like me talking about money. That's when I decided to start Journey to Launch. At first, it was just a blog where I shared my goals and what I was doing with my finances. Once I started sharing how much my husband and I were saving, people started to take notice and they wanted to know how they could do what we were doing. What started as an accountability tool quickly became a platform where I could inspire other people to start their own financial-freedom journeys.

Five years later, I'm a mom of three and I was just able to quit my corporate job to work on Journey to Launch full-time. I have not reached the ultimate goal of financial independence just yet, but I am able to find freedom today because I am more intentional with money. We went from not having clear goals, having no budget, and barely investing, to saving almost half our income for two years right before I quit my job this past year. These next steps that I'm about to share with you have allowed me to find a way to live a good life today while also setting myself and my family up for a good life in the future.

Overview of the Steps
Step 1: Understand Your Why

Step 2: Develop a Positive Money Mind-set

Step 3: Be Committed to Learning (and Give Yourself Grace)

Step 4: Identify Your Goals (Short-, Mid- & Long-term)

Step 5: Create a Budget/Spending Plan

Step 6: Increase Income & Eliminate Unnecessary Expenses

Step 7: Use the Difference Between Your Income & Expenses Toward Your Goals

Step 1: Understand Your Why
Knowing and understanding the "Why" to your story is important in following through on the steps needed to transform your finances. The Why asks you to dig deep within yourself. You need to identify why building wealth and creating financial security is important to you. It's easy to say you know the Why. You may even feel the need to skip this step, but I strongly encourage you not to. Without having a deep connection to the meaning of building wealth, not the cookie-cutter reason "Because I want to buy more things," you will not have a strong sense of purpose and stay committed on the journey.

Your Why doesn't have to be just one thing. It's your story and reason for wanting to push through on the journey when things get tough. Questions to help you find your Why: What are your values? Who are the most important people to you? How does being unhappy or not satisfied in your finances affect you emotionally? What do you want to accomplish by improving your finances? What money lessons did you learn from your parents? Do you want to avoid or repeat them for your children? What kind of financial security do you want to provide for your children?

Step 2: Develop a Positive Money Mind-set
Now that you've written down your Why, the next step is to actually believe that you can build wealth and improve your finances. Often, what most holds you back is not lack of knowledge but your lack of confidence. If you weren't taught basic money-management skills, how can you ever internalize that financial freedom is actually attainable? Financial freedom can seem like an unrealistic goal if you never had any positive financial influences growing up. If you were exposed to the constant cycle of not having enough money and resources to make ends meet, breaking through that ingrained thought process will be scary. You have to first believe that you are worthy of becoming financially free and that it's possible for you to build wealth. Then you have to be willing to change the way you view your self-worth and accomplishments. If you were not shown the value of healthy financial habits, then you may place more value on things versus financial security. This leads to a habit of overcompensating for your lack of self-worth by avoiding your financial issues, and overspending. There's no doubt you deserve it all in life, but there is a caveat that people don't mention when they talk about living the good life: The good life should not come at the cost of your financial security *and* just because it's expensive doesn't mean it's of value to you. The good life is not derived from the type of car you drive, the bag you have, or the type of clothes you wear. Sure, it may make you feel better to adorn yourself with nice and expensive things, but that's all superficial and fleeting. That craving to satisfy your self-worth through material possessions will only put you in a dangerous cycle of consumption. You will keep acquiring things to impress others without ever really filling that void of happiness.

Financial freedom can seem like an unrealistic goal if you never had any positive financial influences growing up.

Step 3: Be Committed to Learning (and Give Yourself Grace)

In order to make the changes and improvements you want to see in your finances, you are going to have to take the initiative to seek out resources and educate yourself on ideas and concepts you are not familiar with. Ask questions, seek answers, and be willing to try new methods when it comes to your finances. Become the CEO (chief educational officer) of your money. Actively work to educate yourself on financial topics by reading blogs, articles, and books. Listen to podcasts to help you grasp financial concepts.

Remember to be patient with yourself. You won't be able to learn everything all at once. It's totally okay if you don't always understand a concept or if you make a mistake on your finance journey. You won't do everything right. You're not meant to be perfect. Give yourself the grace to make mistakes. What matters is that you make an effort to learn from your mistakes and get better.

Step 4: Identify Your Goals (Short-, Mid- and Long-term)

You are more likely to be deterred from reaching success if you don't have clear financial goals. Having goals and knowing why you want to achieve them gives you better resolve to stay on the financial-freedom journey. It's harder to be influenced by temptation and the behaviors of others when you have a clear sense of purpose and goals. Your goals should be written down and visible. It's difficult to turn down buying a pair of fabulous shoes if you don't remember your even-more-fabulous goals.

Your goals should be broken out into four categories: near-term (within 1 year); short-term (1–5 years); mid-term (5–10 years); long-term (10+ years).

Your goals also need to be SMART: specific, measurable, achievable, relevant, and timely. For example, an obscure goal is "I want to save more money." Let's turn that into a SMART goal: "I want to save $2,000 toward my emergency-savings fund in the next six months."

Step 5: Create a Budget and Spending Plan

If you don't already have a budget, it can seem really overwhelming and daunting to start one from scratch. The reality is, it really doesn't have to be that complicated if you break it down into manageable steps.

First

Go through recent bank statements and break down all of your spending into the following four categories:

*Monthly Bills: Things you expect to or have to pay on a monthly basis. It's what you owe to service providers and they are usually set in price. Some examples are rent/mortgage, cell phone bill, cable bill.

*Everyday Expenses: Things that you pay on an ongoing basis throughout the month. It may not be a fixed amount but you know about how much you will spend in these categories throughout the month. They include things like groceries, fuel, and household goods.

*Rainy-Day Funds/Sinking Funds: Things you budget for now but plan to pay for in the future. For example, if you pay your car insurance every six months, you would set aside money every month to pay for that expense when the time comes. These also include putting money away for predictable emergencies, such as car repairs.

*Savings Goals: This should include things you are saving for, such as your emergency fund, car replacement fund, vacation fund, et cetera (things from step 4).

Second

Write down all of your debt balances, their interest rates, and the payments you have been making (essentially everything you owe to someone else, except your mortgage). This includes credit cards, student loans, car notes, and home equity lines of credit.

Third

Allocate your income to each budget line item based on what you have spent on average over the past few months. What do you find? Are you in the red after paying all of your bills? Or is there money left over at the end of the month?

In order to understand where your money is going and how it's working or not working for you, you need to see the actual numbers in front of your face. When things are written down, it makes it not only easier to understand but more real.

Step 6: Increase Income & Eliminate Unnecessary Expenses

Increase Income: Your income is the driving force behind how fast you'll be able to reach your financial goals. The concept is simple: The more money you make and

The concept of financial independence appealed to me because it was what I was searching for most of my life—the ability to do what I wanted, spend time with the people I loved, and enjoy life without having to worry about money.

keep, the faster you'll be able to achieve financial freedom and security. Your income gives you the competitive advantage in the race to wealth, and you're your own opponent. Instead of only focusing on how to cut back on your expenses, you need to find ways to increase your income.

This may mean that you need to ask for a raise or increase your prices as an entrepreneur. Another way is to find a side hustle: Do you have an interest or talent that you can turn into a side hustle? If you are already in a lot of debt or have little financial stability, choose a low-cost side hustle that doesn't require much of an up-front investment, such as babysitting, dog walking, tutoring, or an online business, for instance. A side hustle can also be selling unused items and clothes in your house. There is probably $1,000 worth of stuff in your closet and garage that is useless to you but useful to someone else.

Eliminate Unnecessary Expenses: Usually, we're taught to look at our expenses in one large group. When you're looking to find more money in your budget so that you can save more, pay off debt, et cetera, you may say to yourself, "I can't, because my expenses are too high." But what do your "expenses" include? All expenses are not created equal. There is a big difference between the expenses you need to live and all other expenses. The faster you're able to understand and come to terms with how

you categorize your expenses, the faster you'll be able to optimize your finances. This is the new framework in which you need to view your expenses: mandatory/need expenses versus discretionary/want expenses. The only expenses that are a priority and need to be paid in this part of the wealth formula are the mandatory expenses.

Here are examples of mandatory/need expenses: mortgage/rent; groceries; health insurance; life insurance; work transportation (fuel and tolls); car repairs/maintenance; home maintenance; clothes (minimum amount needed for work); utilities (gas, electricity, water, sewer, trash, et cetera); medical expenses; household goods/toiletries; internet; cell phone; minimum debt payments.

For context, here are a few examples of discretionary expenses: restaurants/fast food; grooming/personal care (hairdresser, nail salon); cable; gym membership.

Ask yourself the following questions when trying to decide if something is a mandatory expense or discretionary expense: Do you need it to survive? Do you need it to maintain your job?

You must learn to prioritize and shift your mind-set from viewing these expenses as necessities. You don't have to give up every discretionary expense, but you do

have to prioritize them and figure out which ones bring you the most happiness and convenience.

If you enjoy going out to eat for lunch every day and spend $10 per day Monday through Friday, cut back to only going out twice a week and save $120 a month.

For example:

$10 x 5 days = $50 a week ($50 x 4 = $200 a month) spent on lunch. Cut back to only two times—$10 x 2 days = $20 ($20 x 4 = $80 a month)—and that equals $120 of savings to go toward debt or goals (like funding your entrepreneurship dreams).

Step 7: Use the Difference Between Your Income Expenses Toward Your Goals

Work toward finding a balance between maximizing your income and reasonably decreasing your expenses. The difference between the two categories, income minus expenses, equals what's left.

Use what's left, or what I like to call "the magic money pot," for splitting between your goals and other discretionary expenses in life. **gc**

Library of Congress Cataloging-in-Publication Data is on file.

ISBN 978-1-57965-862-5

Front cover photograph by Joyce Kim

Design by McCalman.Co
George McCalman, Aliena Cameron

Artisan books are available at special discounts when purchased in bulk for premiums and sales promotions as well as for fund-raising or educational use. Special editions or book excerpts also can be created to specification. For details, contact the Special Sales Director at the address below, or send an e-mail to specialmarkets@workman.com.

For speaking engagements, contact speakersbureau@workman.com.

Published by Artisan
A division of Workman Publishing Co., Inc.
225 Varick Street
New York, NY 10014-4381
artisanbooks.com

Artisan is a registered trademark of Workman Publishing Co., Inc.

Published simultaneously in Canada by Thomas Allen & Son, Limited

Printed in the United States
First printing, April 2019

10 9 8 7 6 5 4 3 2 1